KEYS TO THE HARVEST

To Ted our Spiritual
leader in Christ
    with all spiritual
            blessings in Christ
    Cristiane

Keys to the Harvest

David Lamb

with Melanie Symonds

Hodder & Stoughton
LONDON   SYDNEY   AUCKLAND

First published in Great Britain in 1997
by Hodder and Stoughton
A division of Hodder Headline PLC

The right of David Lamb and Melanie Symonds to be identified
as the Authors of the Work has been asserted by them in
accordance with the Copyright, Designs and Patents Act 1988.

10 9 8 7 6 5 4 3 2 1

A CIP catalogue record for this title is available
from the British Library

ISBN 0 340 67147 5

Typeset by Palimpsest Book Production Limited,
Polmont, Stirlingshire
Printed and bound in Great Britain by
Cox & Wyman Ltd, Reading, Berkshire

Hodder and Stoughton
A division of Hodder Headline PLC
338 Euston Road
London NW1 3BH

CONTENTS

ACKNOWLEDGMENTS

A great big thank you to my heavenly Father and to my wife, Joyce, who believed in me.

Thanks also to Sarah, Simone, Michelle and Helen for countless hours of typing: Helen, God is still waving at you. My heartfelt thanks to Tim Chapman for the group studies and leadership training. Many thanks to Sylvia and to our prayer partners.

Lastly, thanks to Rita McClaughlan, Eddie Tait and Jim 'will fix it': it's finished – Hallelujah!

FOREWORD

God is Lord of the harvest, and this is to be a time of great harvesting, with many people coming into his kingdom, receiving eternal life and being filled with his Holy Spirit. The great commission the Lord gave to his Church commanded Christians to go and make disciples of all nations – not people with a superficial commitment and relationship with Jesus Christ, but believers who would deny themselves, take up their cross and follow him. Jesus told his first disciples that they were to teach new converts 'to obey everything that I have commanded you'.

This, then, is the business of the Church. Every believer is to be a witness and play his or her part in revealing the love and truth of Jesus Christ to the world. Some will be particularly anointed by God to catch the fish, others to care for new converts and lead them to be fruitful in fulfilling God's purposes for their lives. All are to have a deep compassion for those who do not yet belong to Christ, and a longing to see many saved. A passion for souls!

The health of any congregation is seen in the numbers of people being newly saved. Without a steady flow of new Christians, a local fellowship is not addressing the very purposes for its existence: to pray, believe and work for the extension of God's kingdom.

Christians need to have tools to help them to be more

effective in the task of making Jesus known. This book helps to meet that need. Here is practical, down-to-earth-teaching from someone with long experience, not only of evangelising, but also of teaching others to evangelise. The principles taught here have been well-tested, and work!

Books are no substitute for anointing; but anointing is wasted when there is little knowledge of how to apply it. In recent years God has been pouring out rich anointing on his people. Sadly, much of that anointing has not been put to use for the kingdom, despite the fact that it is for this very reason that God empowers his children. So I encourage Christians to read this book and learn how to be a more effective witness for faith in Jesus Christ.

Next to knowing the joy of your own salvation, there is no greater joy than seeing someone else come to faith in Jesus Christ, discovering that they are loved eternally by him.

Colin Urquhart

INTRODUCTION

Twenty-four years ago I received Jesus as my Saviour and Lord, and have had the privilege and honour to minister in 'full-time service' for twenty of those years. It has always been adventurous and fruitful, and at times it has even been dangerous. God truly took a foolish and wild man and made him his ambassador. My wife, Joyce, and I have travelled to more than sixteen countries and preached to thousands upon thousands of people. Hundreds upon hundreds have responded to the gospel message.

Most of the testimonies described in this book happened before I was appointed to 'the office of evangelist'. I was, and still am, just an ordinary believer. Not once did I sit down and think, 'I'll share my faith today.'

Throughout the years, working in Britain and overseas with two London churches and Youth With A Mission (YWAM), my experience has repeatedly proved that evangelism works best as the task of the whole body of Christ.

This book is born out of my desire to see the body of Christ motivated, equipped, multiplying and growing in the art of winning people for Christ; and it is my strong conviction that we can only learn by doing. The Bible shows that the fivefold ministry of Jesus (Eph. 4:11) is to equip and train the saints for ministry. No longer are we just church members or pew-warmers!

The skill of winning converts to Christ is learnt on the job, often through mistakes, sometimes in repentance and tears, and frequently through laughter and adventure. Those who have never made a mistake have never got started. Their idealism and theories may remain intact, but they are still sitting around talking and not doing. God can deal with mistakes and redeem them – but even God cannot use a chair-bound Christian who has got all the right theories on evangelism and church growth, but is not willing to put them into practice.

This book is a compilation of testimony, practical skills and training. I believe thousands will be added to the Church by applying the truths of how these skills have been used to bear fruit in practice.

The book can be used in several ways. First, it can be a straight read for all those who want to be encouraged and inspired to live their lives as Christians. (Just skip the sections at the end of each chapter.)

Secondly, it can be used by individuals to help them, through the Bible readings and meditations at the end of each chapter, to take practical steps to become more effective as witnesses and in outreach.

Thirdly, it can be used as a complete group-teaching course. The group discussion material at the end of each chapter identifies clear and simple goals for the group to achieve. It provides key Scriptures as the basis for the teaching, and to encourage, challenge and build up the faith of group participants. It suggests a number of questions and discussion points that group members need to address, both individually and as a group. It identifies practical things the group can do, both during meetings and subsequently; and it contains suggestions on how to lead a group to achieve lasting results. Groups need to be led by individuals with an understanding and anointing for evangelism, and group members need to read the relevant chapter before the group meets. This material could wake up a whole church!

I have endeavoured to get you launched (or simply re-launched, if you are a Christian who has become discouraged). Once you are on the move, the Holy Spirit will show you how even your mistakes (yes, howlers and all!) can be used to further God's kingdom. God will bless you richly as you attempt to make him known to the world.

My prayer is that the Spirit of wisdom and revelation may rest on you and that you may know him better, because those who know him will achieve mighty feats. This is the day of both intimacy and adventure. God is doing his own timely, powerful thing. A thousand years is like a day to the Lord; what the Church has laboured to do over a thousand years, he can do in a day. That day has arrived! Hallelujah! Fasten your seat belts!

Note: Please note that all the group study material is equally applicable to men and women, even though I have addressed it to men in places. This is simply to avoid unnecessary grammatical complications. (Men and women are equally anointed by God as witnesses and evangelists, and his plan of salvation for the world is totally non-sexist. So I urge you not to let my writing style distract you from rising up as an empowered witness for the kingdom of God.) I have changed the names of some of the true characters, to protect the innocent!

1

IT STARTS IN THE HEART

Many churches and Christians have stopped sharing the gospel, and often Christians describe their spiritual lives as flat and unexciting. 'Something is missing,' they say to me. It is then that I ask them if they are witnessing to others about their faith in Jesus Christ; frequently, the answer is no. In fact, around 90 per cent of Christians in the West are barren, having converted no one to Christ. This is not God's will, for we are commanded to spread the gospel.

The famous actor David Suchet once asked, 'Why are Christians in the West so reticent to talk about Christ?' Yet almost every day I hear reports of major Christian exploits in other parts of the world. New churches are being planted; multitudes are becoming Christians. Churches are growing into thousands and, in some places, hundreds of thousands.

However, growth *is* now being experienced in the United Kingdom, after many years of apparent decline. At last some sections of the Church are beginning to regain strength, shake off apathy, and rise up to fulfil the great commission of Jesus: 'And this gospel of the kingdom will be preached in the whole world as a testimony to all nations, and then the end will come' (Matt. 24:14).

What type of evangelist are you?

The reason why many Christians shrink from evangelism is because they see it as a frightening activity – almost on a par with cold-calling on people to try to sell them double-glazing! Likewise, they expect to receive the same sort of reaction that double-glazing salesmen do! Also, because many Christians feel they are selling a wonderful product to a specialised market, they usually manage to convince themselves that they could not possibly understand this specialised market or the specialised selling techniques that it requires. A vague guilt can then follow when they decide to avoid any type of evangelistic activity, which is a great shame – and a big loss to God's kingdom.

There is no 'right' way of presenting the gospel

I want to stress that there is no single right way of presenting the gospel; we are *not* all called to spread our faith in the same way. When I tell the Bible students that we are going to do some programmed evangelism, visiting door to door or going out on the streets, I find that some cringe while others are twinkling with anticipation!

The confrontational evangelist

Part of the problem with evangelism stems from the fact that most people associate it with one particular style; I call this style 'confrontational evangelism'. This type of evangelism involves the presentation of the gospel 'cold' to strangers, usually in a meeting or on the street. The amount of unknown factors involved terrifies many people; they do not see themselves as the apostle Peter

5

in Acts 2, or another Billy Graham, or Reinhard Bonnke, and there is no reason why they should.

However, that still does not excuse them from ignoring Jesus's command to 'go into all the world'; they may not be called to be an evangelist in the fivefold ministry described in Ephesians 4:11, but everyone has their own special gifts; and I believe that God is longing to use these for greater fruitfulness.

Over the years I have seen many people gain confidence in sharing their faith as they have realised they have special ways of relating to people, and have seen how God has arranged particular times for them to meet certain people *to whom only they could have related.* The following ministries truly encompass the full breadth of the gospel as demonstrated in Isaiah 61:1–3. These people, between them, will provide good news to the poor, freedom for the captive, release from darkness for prisoners, comfort and gladness.

You will know when you have found your style of evangelism, because you will have a sense of release. Here are some of the other evangelistic styles from the Bible that I have seen people happily adopting in the twentieth century.

The friendship evangelist

Statistics tell us that most of those who become Christians do so through 'friendship evangelism'. This is when people reach out to others in love. Friendship wins people's hearts and opens them up to receive the gospel message, but friendship evangelism extracts its own price: are you willing to get involved in people's lives? The strength of the friendship evangelist is in personal relationships. Such people are always warmly interested in others.

Matthew the tax collector was a friendship evangelist; he opened up his home by inviting all his friends to come and hear Jesus. He relied on friendships built up over many years with these men, so they trusted him when he invited them to hear the new rabbi.

Do you know anyone who enjoys long chats, earns people's trust, and quickly communicates on a deep level with others? This type of person will patiently listen to someone else's problems for hour after hour. And if you yourself sometimes suffer from loneliness, this sort of evangelism may well be for you, because the Bible says, 'He who would like a friend must first be a friend.'

So don't drop old friends: bring them to your home, give them some food, and begin to sow seeds of love into your relationship.

The intellectual evangelist (the apologist)

When you invite a friend to a Christian meeting, you will need wisdom as to which meeting your friend should attend – a confrontational evangelist might put them off for life! They might prefer the intellectual or 'apologetics' approach. Apologists are those – like the apostle Paul or Josh McDowell in this century – who use their intellects to persuade people of the truth of the gospel through logic and reason. However, you will need to be well versed in the Scriptures, so that (like Paul) you can maintain your reasoning when in the company of other intellectuals. It is worth noting that when Paul spent two years in Ephesus, signs and wonders happened while he was on his way to argue in the synagogues!

If you are an inquisitive type who enjoys working with ideas and evidence, relax and enjoy this approach. The gospel is not only to be defined by the confrontational evangelists, but also defended by the apologists. God will

7

line up the right people for you to speak to as you use
your natural skills to explain the gospel.

The testimony-giving evangelist

Some are called simply to share their 'testimony' –
in other words, their own personal account of their
conversion to Christianity.

One of the earliest testimonies from Jesus's ministry
comes from the blind man who says stubbornly in the
face of opposition, 'One thing I do know. I was blind
but now I see!' (John 9:25.) Unlike Paul, he does not
use theology to answer his challengers; his gift is to bear
witness to what Jesus has done for him. After all, who
can argue with restored sight?

Your story need not be dramatic; every believer has a
wonderful testimony, simply because they know Jesus.
Salvation is a miracle in itself.

The invitational evangelist

In one American survey, it emerged that 25 per cent of
people will accept a friend's invitation to go to a Christian
meeting. In other words, 'invitational evangelists' have
the knack of inviting others to church! In the Bible, the
Samaritan woman invited her whole town to go and
meet the Messiah, with the result that many believed.
Her enthusiasm was so infectious that she did not need
to spell out the gospel; God used her in that one task.

I have known many invitational evangelists. One night
a converted Hindu brought fifty sailors to church – they
had jumped ship! He lived in the YMCA and was always
bringing people to church from there, but he never wanted
to share the gospel face to face!

Invitational evangelists always have cars full of children and people – you could pray for a minibus for their ministry!

The Dorcas evangelist

This is one of the most important approaches. Dorcas, in the Acts of the Apostles, was always helping people. She was well known for her acts of service, lovingly performed in the name of her Messiah. Mother Teresa is an example of a 'Dorcas evangelist', her aim in Calcutta having been 'to give people dignity before they die'.

God has put Dorcas evangelists in every area of life; they bring food to the sick, mend cars, or do something else that is equally helpful. They can strike up a useful partnership with a 'friendship evangelist'.

How our fear can die

Fear afflicts many who try to witness, and you too may need to face your fear and overcome it. As a new Christian, a very real challenge in this area occurred for me when a young lady approached me at work.

'Please talk to my grandfather,' she sobbed, big tears rolling down her cheeks. I did my best to comfort her. I had helped to nurse her grandfather, Norman, but now he was in a different ward in the hospital, dying. I walked into the dimly lit ward, and as I tried to focus my eyes I was thinking about how I could talk to an old man who was not only dying, but almost stone deaf as well.

I knew that both the charge nurse and the ward orderly disapproved of my chatting to the patients about God.

9

The orderly saw me, but then disappeared out of the ward door. One down, one to go, I thought. 'Oh, Dave,' called the charge nurse, 'would you look after the ward for a few moments?' Then he, too, was gone. Left alone, my courage returned. This was obviously an opportunity created by God. So standing at the bottom of Norman's bed, I shouted, 'Norman, Jesus loves you!' Silence. Not a blink. No sign of recognition. Foolishness and embarrassment engulfed me.

Some of the other patients were already asleep and I was afraid of waking them. Others were listening to me and I wondered what they were thinking. 'Norman, Jesus loves you!' I shouted again and again, getting louder each time. 'Do you want to go to heaven?' Minutes that seemed like hours went by. Slowly, Norman began to show some signs of recognition. 'Will you pray with me?' I asked. His eyes flickered; a softening look on his face said yes. We prayed together, and Norman received Christ into his heart. A few hours later he died. I believe that he went to heaven.

Something negative in me 'died' as I stood shouting at the end of Norman's bed. There are often barriers to overcome in sharing our faith in Christ. This step of raw obedience was a stepping-stone, from the *fear of people* to the *love for people*.

Have you been in a position where you knew God wanted you to speak about him, but tiredness, or even selfishness, confronted you? In my own particular case, the Holy Spirit was about to school me in how to overcome tiredness, in an amazing way.

The red light was flashing on my car dashboard, and suddenly the engine died. The RAC recovery man worked hard and fast, and soon we were on our way with the car chained to the breakdown truck. An 'inner nudge' from the Holy Spirit kept urging me to talk to the RAC man about Jesus, but tiredness wrapped itself around me like a blanket and I started to nod off. I awoke with a start. 'We've taken a wrong turning,' said the RAC man. 'I've never done that before. It will take about forty-five minutes to get back to the other motorway.'

Again came the prompting to share the gospel with him. The Lord seemed to be making it clear that, if I didn't, we would never get to our destination! When I eventually started to talk about Jesus, the RAC man opened up his heart and told me about his wife, who had died the year before. The tangible presence of God's love filled the cab of that truck and was so strong that I knew God was healing that man's broken heart. He became like a long-lost brother as we talked. At our journey's end, we enjoyed a cup of tea together and he departed a very happy man with a brand-new Bible to read.

Often we are reluctant to speak of Jesus because we fear rejection, or we give up too easily. I too have refused to listen to many whom Christ has sent to me. I am so glad that he did not give up on me! Jesus wants us to have that same perseverance with all people. The following story tells of the fruit of perseverance.

A young schoolgirl knocked on a Korean Buddhist's door to tell him about Jesus. He was dying of tuberculosis, and had already called on Buddha to no avail. Now he was calling on the unknown God of the universe to help him. God's answer? A slip of a schoolgirl! In the Korean culture, a man will rarely listen to a 'mere woman'. Not respecting the girl, he harshly ridiculed her and sent her away. She returned every day for a week until finally, because of her tears, he relented and said he would read the Bible and call upon the living God to heal him. He was gloriously saved and healed. His church is now reported to be the largest in the world.

What would have happened if the young girl had not gone to his door, or if she had left feeling hurt and rejected after the first visit? But she had persisted and, like Jesus, sought that Korean man until he surrendered his life to God. His conversion led to over three-quarters of a million people finding Christ.

If you obey Jesus's vital command to 'go', you will experience a joy unlike any other. Charles Spurgeon said, 'Even if I were utterly selfish and had no care for anything but my own happiness, I would choose if I might, under God, to be a soul-winner; for never did I know perfect, overflowing, unutterable happiness of the purest and most enabling order till I first heard of one who had sought and found the Saviour through my means.'

There are many Christians stuck in what I call 'navel-gazing'. They are looking at themselves – looking for sins; looking for faults. Even in 'successful' churches, there can be less than wholehearted commitment to evangelism as a lifestyle. But the purpose of all the blessing we have received in the Western world, and in our churches, is to equip us to work with others creatively and consistently, just like the first messianic body in Acts 2.

Other people are waiting to be made whole, healed and set free *before* they proclaim the good news. But, in Jesus's day, it was as they went forward that they were healed.

Jesus will do the same for you today. Once, when I went out to share my faith with another, it was amazing to discover that the depression I was experiencing had lifted. I am firmly convinced that many would receive the healing and peace of mind they need if only they would stop 'looking in' and would *go* and *do* instead – just as they are: unhealed, weak, inadequate, in whatever condition. Jesus will meet you on the way.

No 'go', no 'lo'!

If you and your church are not reaching out to non-Christians, then you are disobeying Jesus's great command: GO! Jesus said, 'Go, and lo I am with you always.' Someone once said, very aptly, 'No "go", no "lo"!' We want God's presence, power and love to flow through us, but unless we meet the conditions of his own words, we will not experience his life-flow.

The reason the devil wants to muzzle you – to keep your mouth shut – is because the seed, the Word of God, has tremendous power to produce. It is sharper than any two-edged sword. It will produce salvation in others as it has done in you.

Can we agree with Paul's assertion that, 'I am not ashamed of the gospel' (Rom. 1:16)? Jesus himself declared, 'Whoever acknowledges me before men, I will also acknowledge him before my Father in heaven. But whoever disowns me before men, I will disown him before my Father in heaven' (Matt. 10:32–3).

It was a huge relief when I understood that *I* could not save, heal or bless anyone! It was God's power that saved, not my own intelligence or striving. Obedience and a willingness to look foolish was all that God had required of me. Remember, the gospel is the good news about Christ's death and resurrection. It is a demonstration of God's love for each unique individual. Jesus came to heal the broken-hearted; to set the captives free; to bring joy instead of mourning; and a garment of praise instead of a spirit of despair (Isa. 61:1–3). This is the good news to be preached to the poor and to all those in need.

We must begin just where we are. For instance, if we are not even willing to cross the street to witness, there is no point in thinking that we can succeed in another country! Jesus builds on the little things, and if we are faithful in small things he will give us bigger and better things to attain. Sometimes we are so busy with things in our lives – such as our studies, job, family, mortgage, romance and television – that we do not hear the cries of the needy. Our thinking will determine exactly how fruitful we will be when sharing the gospel, because 'As [a man] thinks in his heart, so *is* he' (Prov. 23:7, New King James Version). Ask yourself, 'What do I think? What do I say? What do I do?' The following story reveals the way in which many of us have thought.

A young man once said to Charles Spurgeon, the famous Baptist preacher, 'I am so disappointed that, when I preached, no one got saved.'

'You don't really expect people to get saved, do you?' Spurgeon asked.

'Well, er, no, not really.'

'Young man,' replied Spurgeon, '*that* is why no one was!'

Correct thinking is in line with God's Word, and expects people to be won everywhere. See yourself converting non-Christians, and you will. I do this, and through me God wins souls in most of the places I visit. This does not make me any more special than others; God wants us *all* to think of talking about Jesus whenever we get the opportunity in our daily situations. Jesus lives in you, and his heart is for everyone to be saved and, as you remember this, they will be!

The power of the gospel

The gospel is much more than words – the words are backed up with the power of God: power that produces salvation, healing, and the dead raised to life. We have often complicated the gospel by our Western mind-sets. We have been schooled in scepticism and

14

rationalism from an early age and tend to discount the miraculous.

When I am in Asia and Africa, the mind-set is completely different; it is easy to see the gospel accompanied by healing and miracles – and, thanks be to God, this has now started to happen in the Western world. This wonderful Jesus we serve has allowed me the privilege to see the miraculous with my own eyes.

When I was a new Christian working in a large geriatric hospital, one of the first people I ever prayed for was a man who had suffered a stroke that had resulted in weakness in his left arm and leg. Arthur was a cheerful old man and I liked him immediately. As an orphan, he had been brought up in one of the George Muller homes in Bristol. He told me that he firmly believed in God, having seen many miracles happen through prayer in the home. When he was twelve, he left the orphanage to become an apprentice to a Jewish tailor. I told Arthur of my conversion and often urged him to accept Jesus into his life, but each time he would say, 'I believe in the God of Abraham, Isaac and Jacob. Why must I go through Jesus when I can go directly to the Boss?'

Over the next twelve months, I got to know Arthur better and found that he was sad, hurt and fearful. He had never recovered from his wife's death and he wanted to die himself. Once, before I met him, he had been resuscitated after a heart attack and had asked the doctor, 'Why don't you let me die?' The doctor replied, 'God has a reason for keeping you alive.' Arthur eventually got a chest infection that made him very ill, and my heart ached as he wasted away while I nursed him. One night, when death was imminent, I could stand it no longer. Yes, Arthur believed in God, but that was not enough. He needed to accept God's loving answer to sin: Jesus. In my room, kneeling by my bed, I prayed, 'Father, you must do something.' The time passed. I do not know how

15

long I stayed there, but suddenly I knew in my heart that God had heard my prayer and that something was indeed happening to Arthur.

The next morning, as I helped to give Arthur his daily blanket bath, he turned to me with wide eyes and whispered, 'I believe in Jesus.' Tears filled his eyes as he knew how great his sins were. 'David,' he said, 'I have done so much wrong. How can God accept me now when I am old?' 'Whoever comes to Jesus, he will not turn him away,' I replied. After prayer, Arthur's face was aglow and he radiated peace. He had found the Saviour of the World – Jesus. Then Arthur really amazed me. 'I have one thing I want to ask God. I want to walk again.' His hand gripped mine as we prayed together, 'Father, we come to you in Jesus's name, asking you to heal and grant this request to walk again.'

Arthur began to recover, first being able to drink, then to eat and sit up. Within three months, he was walking around and attending occupational therapy sessions. On seeing this, the local doctor enthused, 'This is a miracle!' How wonderful to witness a miracle from God with my own eyes. That once partially paralysed, dying man recovered so well that, looking fit, tanned and thoroughly enjoying life, he was able to leave the geriatric hospital and live in a nursing home near his son. Arthur enjoyed many years of peace and joy, and loved going to church with me. He was a changed man, but then that's because of his magnificent Saviour, Jesus.

Each person is unique, so different approaches are needed. Many have broken hearts and will not listen until God's power has healed them first, so that they may then be open to hearing the rest of the good news. It is never good to use the same method for everybody. Jesus, for example, used the 'word of knowledge' and the 'gift of prophecy' while talking to the woman at the well (John 4:7). With Zacchaeus, Jesus first offered his friendship

16

(Luke 19:5). The man at the pool of Bethesda was first healed of his physical disease and only later did Jesus speak to him about his sin (John 5:1–14). Jesus always treated people as individuals with different needs, and approached each one accordingly. We can also do this as we believe that we hear and respond to his voice as he directs our paths.

Winning souls for Christ is a skill to be learnt not only in an intellectual way, but while 'on the job' itself, because practice increases skill. Let me give you an example. When you start to drive a car, there are so many things to do that it appears impossible at first. However, as you practise you soon find out that it becomes second nature.

Where will you be in ten years' time? What will you do with your life? It is the best gift you have. Give it to God and let him make it count in blessings to multitudes.

The cause is urgent. Every generation has believed it was living in the end-times, ever since the apostle John warned of the coming of the antichrist as a sign of 'the last hour' (1 John 2:18). How much more now, nearly two thousand years later, should we sense an urgency to fulfil the great commission and see non-believers won to Christ.

The Bible promises that when the full number of Gentiles has come into the kingdom, 'all Israel will be saved' (Rom. 11:25–6), and the Messiah will return to his land (Zech. 12:10, 14:3–4). With Jerusalem back in Jewish hands since 1967, we have the evidence Jesus spoke of in Luke 21:24, that the times of the Gentiles are fulfilled. It is interesting to note that the charismatic movement came alive after 1967. The prosperity of the Church has often reflected the state – both national and spiritual – of Israel.

How much more compelling evidence do we need to

17

finish the work Jesus set us? Jesus said that he would not return until everyone had heard the gospel (Matt. 24:14). We can either hasten or delay our Lord's second coming. This is a real challenge!

All evangelism starts in the heart. What our hearts are set on is that which will motivate us and galvanise us into action. God loves the lost; all that is within him cries out for their salvation. As we become more like our God, our deep yearning will be like his. When our hearts are tender in this way, we will win souls for Christ

The stories I will share with you are all true events. They show how the God of grace helped me to face fears and overcome them.

Let's be people who have a lifestyle of witnessing – and not just when on an outreach or when we think we should do it! This book is to help you get started in evangelism, no matter how impossible it seems. Keep on working with God until it becomes second nature, then it will soon become your lifestyle. Start where you can and God will take you where you could not go, to do what you could not do.

FOR FURTHER THOUGHT

• Meditate on the following Scriptures:
    Romans 1:14–17
    Matthew 10:32–3
    John 15:1–8

• Ask yourself:
    Am I always ready to share the gospel?
    What might prevent me from sharing the gospel?
    What are my expectations of success when I share the gospel with non-Christians?

• Prayer:
    Father, forgive my fear, my lack of zeal and

expectation. Please fill my heart with a new love for you and with high expectations of what you will do through me by your Holy Spirit. Please give me your heart for the lost, and many 'divine appointments' so that I may be fruitful in winning many souls for your glory. Amen.

FOR GROUP DISCUSSION

Aim of the chapter
By the end of the meeting, participants will:

1 Have identified where there is a need for them to seek a change of heart, and asked God to accomplish this change.

2 Have found out which form of evangelism suits them.

3 Have discovered the breadth of the gospel as illustrated in Isaiah 61:1–3.

4 Realise afresh the urgency of fulfilling the great commission.

Key Scriptures
Read and meditate on the following Scriptures. Underline or make a note of verses that particularly speak to you.

1 *Romans 1:14–17:* I am bound both to Greeks and non-Greeks, both to the wise and the foolish. That is why I am so eager to preach the gospel also to you who are at Rome. I am not ashamed of the gospel, because it is the power of God for the salvation of everyone who believes: first for the Jew, then for the Gentile. For in the gospel a righteousness from God is revealed, a righteousness that is by faith from first to last, just as it is written: 'The righteous will live by faith.'

2 *Matthew 10:32–3:* Whoever acknowledges me before men, I will also acknowledge him before my Father in heaven. But whoever disowns me before men, I will disown him before my Father in heaven.

3 *Isaiah 61:1–3:* The Spirit of the Sovereign LORD is on me, because the LORD has anointed me to preach good news to the poor. He has sent me to bind up the broken-hearted, to proclaim freedom for the captives and release from darkness for the prisoners, to proclaim the year of the LORD's favour and the day of vengeance of our God, to comfort all who mourn, and provide for those who grieve in Zion – to bestow on them a crown of beauty instead of ashes, the oil of gladness instead of mourning, and a garment of praise instead of a spirit of despair. They will be called oaks of righteousness, a planting of the LORD for the display of his splendour.

4 *Jeremiah 32:17:* Ah, Sovereign LORD, you have made the heavens and the earth by your great power and outstretched arm. Nothing is too hard for you.

5 *Psalm 23:6:* Surely goodness and love will follow me all the days of my life, and I will dwell in the house of the LORD for ever.

6 *Mark 16:17:* And these signs will accompany those who believe: In my name they will drive out demons; they will speak in new tongues; they will pick up snakes with their hands; and when they drink deadly poison, it will not hurt them at all; they will place their hands on sick people, and they will get well.

7 *John 15:1–8:* I am the true vine, and my Father is the gardener. He cuts off every branch in me that bears no fruit, while every branch that does bear fruit he prunes so that it will be even more fruitful. You are already clean because of the word I have spoken to you. Remain in me, and I will remain in you. No branch can bear fruit by itself; it must remain in the vine. Neither can you bear fruit unless you remain in me. I am the vine; you are the branches. If a man remains in me and I in him, he will bear much fruit; apart from me you can do nothing. If anyone does not remain in me, he is like a branch that is thrown away and withers; such branches are picked up, thrown into the fire and burned. If you remain in me and my words remain in you, ask whatever you wish, and it will be given you. This is to my Father's glory, that you bear much fruit, showing yourselves to be my disciples.

Group participation
Respond individually and as a group (as appropriate) to the following questions/prompting:

1 Am I ready and willing to share the gospel? What are the ways to overcome fear?

2 What are my expectations of fruitfulness when I share the gospel with non-Christians?

3 Look at Isaiah 61:1–3 again. Reflect for three to four minutes on the breadth of the gospel, then discuss.

4 Discuss which form of evangelism suits you best: confrontational, friendship, intellectual (the apologist), testimony-giving, invitational, or the Dorcas evangelist (the person who testifies to people through good deeds).

5 Your thoughts and words reflect your heart attitude. Be honest. What thoughts and words have flowed from you recently that reveal heart attitudes (towards non-believers and fellow Christians) that need to change if you are to become more effective as a witness?

Prayer
Pray as a group and individually (as appropriate):

1 Pray aloud on the themes of Isaiah 61:1–3.

2 Turn the John 15:1–8 Scripture into a prayer. Praise God for who he is, and for what he is/has done/will do. Proclaim these truths over your own life and ministry. Thank God that you have a 'ministry'. (The gospel calls all Christians 'ministers of the gospel' not 'members of the Church'!) Intercede for yourself and others.

Action
1 Each group member should tell their neighbour (or in front of the whole group if it is small):
    (a) What wrong heart attitudes they have asked the Lord to change, and what they have asked God to replace them with.
    (b) Which non-Christians they want to witness to in the near future, and what they believe will be accomplished when they do speak to them.
    (c) What the main lessons are that they have learnt through reading the chapter and the group session.

2 When you get home, make a list of the following: friends and past friends; business contacts (past and present); people you have promised to contact in the past, but have not done so yet. Mark against each name whether you will phone them, or write them a personal letter, to let them know what you are up to. You don't always need to witness immediately, but look for opportunities to witness as you (re-)establish contact with them. Typical opportunities that will crop up include inviting them: to a meal or party; to watch a video; to go with you to the cinema/a football match/an evening class.

Suggestions for Group Leaders
• As this is the first time the group has met, you need to allow time for group members to get to know each other. Let every person introduce themselves aloud, share their

experience of witnessing, and their particular reasons for wanting to become more effective Christian witnesses.

• Encourage those who are successful in their witnessing to talk about what God has said to them about their calling to witness. Get a feel for personality types, and who to encourage to speak and who to discourage!

• Each week, you need to work through the chapter and 'do' the group session before leading the group. You should also seek the Lord for understanding of how individuals will react to the message contained.

• In this and subsequent meetings, use the 'Aim of the Chapter' headings to introduce the meeting and what it will accomplish. Make sure that everyone understands and wants to achieve these aims.

• You should be especially sensitive to embarrassment about wrong heart attitudes and a reluctance to confess what may be seen as shameful or embarrassing faults and weaknesses. Encourage individuals to be honest and open, by being the first to open up to the group about the state of your own heart and weaknesses.

• Look out for any undue emphasis on confessing faults. Keep the focus on 'the positive confession'. (God is more interested in what we have faith for seeing him do in us and through us, than with what is wrong with us – which he knows anyway!) Take every opportunity to encourage and embolden group members.

• Seek to bring people back to the Word of God whenever they show a tendency to 'live in' (that is, put more faith in) their feelings and experiences rather than God's promises. (Our feelings usually fall short of God's words and promises for his people.) Sensitively and gently, challenge each group member to come back afresh to God's word. Isaiah 61 is packed with marvellous promises and instruction about God's view of his people and the gospel we proclaim in word and deed. Encourage those who feel anxious about witnessing, or who feel they have failed in the past, not to settle for their past negative experiences. Let the word of God lift them up to his level and inspire them with his vision for their ministries. (Don't bring the Word of God down to the level of past experiences!)

• Help the group to become confident in praying aloud, both individually and as a group. It is an experience of churches moving into revival that corporate praying (even unabashed and noisy corporate praying!) becomes the norm when the church meets. There is nothing wrong with twenty (or more) people all praying different words out loud at the same time, so long as the words are all flowing in the same direction, under the direction of the Holy Spirit. (Where it is important for one person to be heard above the rest of the group [for example, so that others can agree with what is being prayed and detect and move with changes in the Spirit's direction], charismatic groups can pray in tongues – but quietly enough for the person praying to still be heard.)

• When there are actions that the group can usefully take after the meeting – whether our notes specify what they are or are not – make a point of encouraging participants to do them.

It is only in action between meetings that the gospel will be proclaimed. And, if group members haven't overcome their natural reluctance to witness before the end of the course, the odds are rather long that they will have the courage to act at a later date!

2

A BURNING COMPASSION

For the first twenty-five years of my life, I swallowed the lie that God did not exist. My picture of a Christian was of a weak, skinny, pimply and bespectacled individual who was over-earnest and humourless. Television programmes presented wimpish, ineffectual vicars or bishops who had few or no beliefs; they were the butt of coarse jokes and ridicule. That was my indoctrination by an unbelieving, secular media.

A vision of Jesus

At twenty-five, though, my outlook changed. God gave me a dream (in technicolour!) in which I met Jesus. It was, and still is, powerfully clear to me. I was sitting in a huge crowd of people listening, enthralled, as Jesus taught us. I can remember the woven, colourful tunics and the intrigued, excited atmosphere.

Then it happened; he stopped teaching and looked at me. As he gazed directly into my eyes, I knew that he loved me with a depth of love that I had never experienced before. I was also aware that he knew my hidden sin, but that still he did not reject me.

Revelation of love

The love I experienced through that dream swept away the years of deception, and ensured that thereafter I believed in God. If only people knew the true Jesus – holy, majestic, loving, bold, a true radical hero, someone who was unafraid to speak of justice. I believe that most people would not have a problem in accepting Jesus or his teachings; instead, they have a problem with the *persona* the Church has given him.

Thank God we are beginning to live in an age when Christians are no longer being viewed as wimps, but as true champions of Jesus. Politicians, actors, sports personalities, musicians, the rich, the poor, Asians, blacks and whites – all are beginning to declare their allegiance boldly.

Knowing Jesus is not about following a set of rules or a code of behaviour; it's about intimate, gutsy, gentle, firm love. Jesus is what society might call a 'man's man', someone whom men, as well as women and children, can follow with confidence.

He was one of the first people I met who didn't have a 'hidden agenda' – otherwise known as selfishness. Human nature is such that we often give something in order to receive something in return. I had been cheated on and lied to for many years, and had lied to and cheated on others.

Only when I allowed God to love me did I truly begin to live. For as long as I could remember, I had struggled with hatred in my heart. However, the day after my surrender to Jesus, I awoke to discover the hatred had vanished. To this day, I don't know how it happened – it was the first miracle I experienced as a believer!

No one told me you had to go to church or that you had to tell others about Christ. But when the church opened, I was there. Everyone needed to know this love, and I told everyone who would listen.

Burning compassion

I knew my sins were gross and I deserved punishment, but God granted me mercy and forgiveness instead. Through this outpouring of love, I knew he had a burning compassion for the world, which was now burning in me as well. How I loved God and loved people! 'We love because he first loved us' (1 John 4:19).

So why are there so many unproductive, fearful Christians? I believe it is because they are not convinced that God really does love them. But God's love decrees no more punishment or torment for those who believe in Jesus because 'perfect love drives out fear' (1 John 4:18).

The knowledge that we are God's very own children, unconditionally loved, gives us boldness before him. And if you are bold before God, you will be bold before men, just as Jesus was. Don't be tempted to say, 'I need to experience more of his love before I can talk about it.' Rather, share what you have with those who have nothing. We all know what it is to be ruled by the cycle of up-and-down feelings and moods; now it's time to live by the truth. You know that God so loved you that he sent Jesus to die on the cross for you. Say to yourself every day, 'God loves me, I am accepted,' and picture the embrace of Jesus.

The secret of great soul-winners

Great soul-winners are those who have tasted the love of God and know that they are redeemed from God's just and deserved anger. In awe and wonder at his grace towards them, they are compelled to tell others about that love; that was how I reacted to finding out about Jesus. 'Her many sins have been forgiven – for she loved much' (Luke 7:47). 'For the wages of sin is death, but the gift of God is eternal life in Christ Jesus our Lord' (Rom. 6:23).

Warning others about hell

Lately, it has occurred to me that those who end up in hell could accuse us of never warning them of this dreadful place. This accusation would be justified, for, without the whole truth, how could they have made a fully informed choice?

The Bible clearly states that there is a location called 'hell'. Those who do not receive Christ and follow him will go there. It is a place of torment. Hell, Satan, demons and people will be cast into the lake of fire and tormented day and night for ever and ever following the Last Judgment (Rev. 20:11–15). This is what the Bible says; it is very different from saying that God will never send anyone to hell and that everyone will be forgiven in the end.

Imagine heaven with its inexpressible beauty, full of love, joy, peace and harmony, with the world as God created it reflecting this harmony. It is a fact that man's sin has brought the earth down to only a shadow of its former glory, and man himself, who was created in God's image, has become depraved, selfish and arrogant.

God could have risen in judgment, but he had a master plan: 'For God so loved the world that he gave his one and only Son, that whoever believes in him shall not perish but have eternal life' (John 3:16). Mercy triumphed over deserved judgment. God sent Jesus, who left the splendour, love, beauty, harmony and comfort of heaven

to come to this sad, sick world. He took off his roy
and kingly glory. He who was rich became poor fc
sakes. He who knew no suffering, came to suffer untold
agonies and death at the hands of humanity.

What was it that brought him down from the joy of
heaven to the sadness of earth? *It was an immeasurable
love for the lost.* How many are lost? The Bible declares
that 'all have sinned and fall short of the glory of God'
(Rom. 3:23). Sin pays its own wages: death (Rom. 6:23).
This means eternal separation from a loving God; eternal
condemnation to the fiery torment of hell itself. The book
of Revelation tells of death and hell as being thrown into
a lake of fire where all the inhabitants will be tormented
day and night for ever. Imagine the horror of living with
Satan for eternity. That's torment!

Let me clarify again exactly who is lost; it is all those
who do not have a personal, intimate relationship with
Jesus Christ. 'Whoever believes in him is not condemned,
but whoever does not believe stands condemned already
because he has not believed in the name of God's one
and only Son' (John 3:18). All are lost who have not
turned away from their sin and accepted his forgiveness
and cleansing (1 John 1:9).

Jesus cried for his people; I believe we are closer to him
if we, too, cry for the lost. Let's not be ashamed of tears;
after all, the fear of 'letting go in public' is only a fear in
our Western culture; if the Prime Minister of Israel shed
tears, his people would say 'What a man!', but if the President of the United States wept, people would think he was
unhinged and would want to remove him from office!

In the parable of the lost sheep, the shepherd (Jesus)
left the safe ones, ninety-nine of them, to rescue only
one (Luke 15:3–7). It cost him time, energy and sacrifice
to reach the lost one. Do you love the lost enough to
inconvenience yourself?

One preacher revealed how he had prayed for years to

have a deep compassion for others, but never seemed to experience it. In desperation he cried out to God, 'Let me see the lost as you see them.' God, of course, answered him. The preacher was forced to stop the car to watch passing faces, with tears spilling down his face and, I hasten to add, he was changed for ever by this experience.

Ask God for a deep love for your city, town, neighbourhood, work colleagues and family. Turn complaints into prayer for non-believers. Go beyond the comfort, clique-level of fellowship. Act, reach out, take the risk, smile, speak and, most importantly, love. People will notice; they always do. Once I tried an experiment in prayer, with the following words: 'Lord, please love the children through me. Amen.'

Amazing things began to happen. The children at church climbed over me, held my hand, got healed, became quiet, some even fell asleep. In this we see the power of God and his response to our prayers. Jesus loved children. You cannot fool youngsters; they know who is real and who is a phoney. The children came to Jesus. They will not go to a misery, to someone who is always heavy-handed with them, judging them. So, from this perspective, neither will non-Christians! Sinners followed Jesus in their crowds. Why? Because of love. You can pray now to make God's love flow through you. People will sense it; and you will find them as the Holy Spirit leads. Love *never* fails. God's love *always* conquers, and you really are more than a conqueror in Christ, through his perfect love. The love of God compelled the apostle Paul to preach and suffer for Christ. The same love will compel us to leave the ninety-nine and go after the lost one.

Finding the lost sheep

Martina, a young teenage girl, asked me to visit her at

home. She had been coming to church, but was now in some serious trouble. If I could, I wanted to help. As my wife, Joyce, and I came into the dark hallway of Martina's house, the stench of urine hit me. Filthy children were everywhere, fighting, banging, shouting. It was mayhem.

Inside, Martina's portly mother invited us to sit on an over-sized grimy chair. It felt like something out of a novel by Charles Dickens. 'Would you like a cup of tea, m'lad?' Martina's mother asked. 'Yes, yes please,' I replied. The cup was cracked and unwashed, and I prayed before I gulped down the sweet brew. Nausea arose from deep within me as the awful smells blended potently to attack my senses. 'Share my love with them. Speak about me,' urged the Holy Spirit inside me. My wife caught my eye; her body language seemed to be saying. 'Let's get out of here.' But as soon as I started to talk about God's love, the words bubbled out of me and I instantly became oblivious to the smells. This dear lady was drinking it all in and hanging on to every word.

Martina's mother had never heard the gospel before. But she was now sitting at her Lord's feet, with his love flowing to her. Before I left that day, we bowed our heads and she prayed the sinner's prayer to receive Christ. The joy and fulfilment for Joyce and me were beyond words.

God had used us to seek out this woman, because he values the one who is on their own and lost. His value system is the very opposite of the world's values. Position, fame and money have a high profile in our society, and outward appearance affects the rewards we receive from the world; it has even been proved that those whom the world sees as good-looking have better-paid jobs!

God's values

But God loves and values just one person above all the

31

world's riches. Would we be able to say that our values are God's values? We could, if we realised that earthly position and wealth are to be held lightly and no expense spared to bring just one lost person home to God.

We Christians must understand that the human heart without Christ is utterly bankrupt, without any goodness and destined for eternal judgment. Many can be bewitched by the illusion that everything will be all right in the end, but, sadly, this is deception.

You will not be motivated to win souls for Christ unless you know you were doomed without Jesus and are now totally safe and pardoned by him. Unless you are convinced that all are lost without Christ, you will not have the urgency to go in love and pursue them.

The great media lie

In twenty years of ministry, I have preached one sermon on hell – the place where the unsaved go when they die. In twenty-four years of Christianity, I have heard one sermon on hell. I have mentioned the word 'hell' on numerous occasions in my preaching, but not as a clear biblical teaching.

Predominantly through ridicule, the media have done a good job of banishing any fear of hell from the minds of the population at large. The word 'hell' brings different impressions into people's minds. It may be mockery, sheer disbelief, the idea that this earth is hell enough, or that hell is a burning fire where really evil people go, but not ordinary mortals.

This latter belief is still held by some Christians, and it is important that we should each be convinced about the fate of 'good' people. Many Christians meet 'good' members of other religions, and want to believe that they will be saved on account of their good deeds. 'They don't know the Lord, not having heard the gospel, so surely God has a place for them?' they reason. Cornelius the centurion did not know the Lord, even though he was doing good deeds, so God had to send somebody, Peter, to tell him the gospel, so that Cornelius might go to heaven on dying.

Volunteers, not soldiers

While the general population has discounted hell, the Church has also let itself be swayed by the popular mood, presenting a less challenging interpretation of eternal truth. Sadly, this sugar-coated gospel has produced selfish believers, a 'Bless Me Now Club', which results in the churches being full of volunteers rather than obedient soldiers. Church is not a long-term hospital; the sooner believers understand that it represents spiritual barracks, the better for the spread of the gospel!

Drifting off to meetings for a supernatural experience is a million light years away from the true gospel: 'and anyone who does not take up his cross and follow me is not worthy of me. Whoever finds his life will lose it, and whoever loses his life for my sake will find it' (Matt. 10:38–9). I have nothing against genuine supernatural experiences, but these experiences will always produce real fruit; they are not an end in themselves. In Acts 2, when the Holy Spirit is poured out to empower the disciples and 3,000 accept Peter's message of the Messiah on that one day, we see that supernatural events precede salvation and repentance.

The Jews were also prepared for the presentation of the gospel because God's dealings with them through Moses and the prophets had always emphasised repentance, whose root means turning (back to their God). Now the expectation of a Messiah, briefly disappointed through Jesus's death, was reawakened by Peter's teaching at

Pentecost. Peter explained that the manifestations of the outpouring of the Holy Spirit was a fulfilment of Joel's prophecy:

> And afterwards,
> I will pour out my Spirit on all people.
> Your sons and daughters will prophesy,
> your old men will dream dreams,
> your young men will see visions.
>
> (Joel 2:28; Acts 2:17)

After hearing him explain how God was moving among them and the time they were now in, Peter's listeners understood that *they had to respond to God's message through the apostles* in order to be saved from what was coming on earth. Peter also pleads with them to 'Save yourselves from this corrupt generation'. (To be 'saved' has the meaning of 'being delivered'.)

Thus they asked the apostles, 'Brothers, what shall we do?' The reply was, 'Repent, every one of you.' I have been asked this question by some in Africa – in Kenya – but not in the West, where the spiritual climate is very different. In Kenya they have experienced a revival from Rwanda, a move of God that was accompanied by repentance and restitution (asking for forgiveness, giving back stolen property, and restoring broken relationships).

Let the terror of the Lord – that is, the knowledge of what will happen to them – spur you on to tell them of Christ. Paul said, 'Since, then, we know what it is to fear the Lord, we try to persuade men' (2 Cor. 5:11). Paul knew what end awaits the non-believer. He loved them and was willing to love and suffer to help them (2 Cor. 11:22–33).

A fresh stress on true repentance is needed, not in a patronising, self-righteous way nor a heavy condemning manner, but with the truth spoken in love.

Does your doctrine need doctoring?

Tragically, we often hear a 'gospel' that stresses only the benefits of accepting Christ, rather than the penalty of denying him. In twenty-one years of Christian life, I have overheard many friendly suggestions along the lines of, 'Why don't you just give Jesus a try? He solved my problems. He will help you. He gave me love, joy and peace. Try him and see for yourself.'

What has happened to the doctrine of repentance? I am convinced that a sensitive and wise exposition of the doctrine of repentance is essential for a true conversion, together with an explanation of the contrast between eternal life and eternal judgment.

This does not contradict power evangelism as, very often, God will use the miraculous to get someone's attention. After the miraculous, though, it is vital that we present the full gospel of Jesus Christ. Paul said, 'So be on your guard! Remember that for three years I never stopped warning each of you night and day with tears' (Acts 20:31), and, 'For I have not hesitated to proclaim to you the whole will of God' (Acts 20:27).

It is then that your hearers will be able to balance the benefits of Christianity with the consequences of refusal: the wrath of God that is coming to the whole world. Judgment is coming upon the ungodly, those who do not accept Christ. God said, 'You shall have no other gods before me' (Exod. 20:3). 'Other gods' include materialism, money, pop idols, football, relationships with husband, wife, boy/girl friend, career, sex and drugs. 'No other gods' means exactly that. We cannot follow the Saviour unless we truly forsake our old life's goals, repent and trust in him alone. The only way to escape judgment is to follow the Saviour, Jesus Christ.

Charles Finney was noted for preaching repentance as

well as the grace and love of God, and it is said that 80 per cent of his converts continued as disciples of the Lord. But I have seen those who decided to 'try' Jesus, like spiritual consumers, in their search for love, joy and peace. Most of these people came into church, stayed a while, then left, disgruntled, saying. 'You never told me it would be like this! I've been persecuted and misunderstood since I got into religion. I'm off!' They would then go, usually never to be reached again.

Let us, wisely and sensitively, present the full gospel – the benefits and implications of our choice. Try not to rush. Let the person come to a genuine conviction with a measured response to the truth. As a result, our new believers will stay soundly converted, becoming genuine disciples and living in the fear of the Lord. Arthur, mentioned in Chapter 1, was one of these. I talked to him as often as possible over a year, but he was not ready to receive Christ until he fully understood the message. Once he understood, he made a great disciple and a wonderful witness, because he was 'fully persuaded'.

Persecution

Anyone who preaches the true gospel has to be prepared for adverse reactions and rejection. Jesus said, 'If they persecuted me, they will persecute you also. If they obeyed my teaching, they will obey yours also' (John 15:20b).

If you are not being persecuted, ask yourself if you are compromising your message – or perhaps you are not presenting Jesus at all? Because it is natural to recoil from any sort of rejection, we often water down our message to make it more acceptable. Praise God that many do receive the message and become disciples of the Lord Jesus.

Test your testimony

Always make full use of your testimony, your own story of becoming a Christian. Jesus tells us to have our testimony always ready. It is very difficult for people to argue with a true story, especially when it is your own; the apostle Paul often used his testimony. A testimony is one of the most powerful tools we have (Rev. 12:11) – and beware of falling into the trap of saying, 'But I don't have a powerful testimony.' Some people can relate to dramatic conversions, but you can be sure that others will be drawn to Jesus by the story of gentle or gradual entry into God's kingdom. Remember that the greatest miracle has happened to you! You know the Lord personally; you are his child and he lives in you, whether or not you remember the day you accepted him. Talk like a son or daughter of the King of kings, and introduce your friends to Jesus the King. After all, it is the greatest gift that you have to give to anyone. Don't hide your light – let it shine!

How to share your story with non-Christians

Sadly, most Christians haven't a clue as to how they should share their story with a non-believer. After hearing some testimonies where the speaker talks about his life of sin in detail, only adding at the end that he received Jesus, I have often wondered who was being glorified.

My advice is to be very general about the past. Only give an overview and leave your in-depth detail for the listener who is really ready and wants to hear. Try to use words that create pictures in the minds of those listening, just as Jesus did. He used images of sowing and reaping, wind and fire, sheep and shepherds – all things familiar

37

to his listeners. We should follow his great example and relate to this generation while using mid-1990s parables! If there was sexual sin, no detail is required. For example, you could say, 'Before I knew Jesus, I was driven by lust, but since I met Jesus, I've totally changed and it feels so good.'

Work on your story. Write it out in long hand, then summarise and shorten it. Get another friend to evaluate it to make it relevant to the hearer; it doesn't need to be word perfect.

When prompted, tell your story, but be selective, highlighting certain portions. On occasions it will be appropriate to tell the whole story – you will know this by the listener's attention span. Someone with whom you are on friendly terms will probably be prepared to listen longer than three minutes, but people you have just met are unlikely to give you longer:

• *First minute*: Explain what you were like before you became a Christian. Generalise: 'I felt bad about my way of life before I became a Christian.'

• *Second minute*: Tell what happened when you met Christ. For example: 'When I came to know Jesus personally, it happened like this . . .'

• *Third minute*: Talk about one important thing you are experiencing now as a Christian. For example, 'God is taking me on such an exciting journey/I have such peace in my heart every day.'

Junk the jargon!

When you write your testimony, bear in mind that you will be speaking to people who do not know anything about Christianity, and you need to be ruthless in weeding out jargon. Sometimes people latch on to Christian jargon as a kind of spiritual shorthand that will help them relate instantly to other believers and feel at home in their new circle.

Doesn't this strike you as somewhat strange? The gospel was never meant to have its own language like a secret society. Let's not forget what Jesus demonstrated as a master teacher and communicator; he successfully brought the character and love of God to his people by using language they would have understood.

Two thousand years later, the United Kingdom is a largely secular society, so it is utterly pointless for Christians to bandy about religious jargon when those terms are not common currency. Your aim is to attract people – not to alienate them by using an exclusive language.

The terms Jesus used were conventional rabbinical terms that all the Jewish people would have understood; in other words, he spoke in everyday Hebrew. Some examples of this are as follows: 'repent' was a popular topic among the Pharisees in Jesus's time – everyone knew it meant turning from your sin back to the Lord; 'deliverance' – rabbis practised casting out evil spirits (Jesus was the first rabbi to heal a man who was born blind); 'bind and loose' – this means to permit or forbid (a rabbi would permit or forbid someone to do something according to his interpretation of Torah, the teaching of Moses); 'the kingdom of heaven' – (this was a reverent way of referring to the Lord himself; his name was holy above all things and was not used casually).

Jargon list

Try to use the 'translations' of the following Christian jargon:
- *To share* = to speak, tell, say
- *To be saved* = to become a Christian

- *Testimony* = experience (as a Christian)
- *A brother/sister in the Lord* = a Christian friend
- *To fellowship/have fellowship* = spend time with other Christians
- *'I was spending a lot of time in the Word'* = 'I was reading my Bible a lot'
- *'I was in the flesh'* = 'I wasn't at all spiritually minded'
- *'The Lord told me to share with you'* = 'I thought I'd come and talk to you.' If what you have to say is of God, you will see results that glorify him. If it is not, you will have brought his name into disrepute by saying, 'The Lord told me . . .' Jesus never justified his actions by saying, 'God told me to come and heal you' – he just went!
- *'These mature brothers came alongside me and really ministered to me in areas of my life where I needed a breakthrough'* = 'Some people who had been Christians for many years took the time to pray with me and help me over my problems'
- *'He's really going on with the Lord'* = 'He is maturing in his faith/becoming a strong believer'
- *'He's got a great testimony about being delivered from alcoholism'* = 'He had an amazing experience of being able to give up drinking after asking God to help him'
- *'My sin was weighing me down'* = 'I began to feel bad about my way of life'

If in doubt, watch a programme like BBC1's *Songs of Praise*, in which people speak of their faith in a straightforward fashion, or read *Challenge*, an evangelistic newspaper that is full of de-jargonised testimonies.

SUMMARY

Essential ingredients for wanting to evangelise:

• A firm understanding that *every* non-Christian is lost for ever (Rev. 20:1–15; John 3:18).
• A deep love for non-believers (Luke 19:39–44; Acts 4:15–20).
• Obedience to God's command to *go*! (Matt. 28:19–20).

FOR GROUP DISCUSSION

Aim of the Chapter
By the end of the meeting, participants will:

1 Know the foundation of the Christian faith: God is love; I am totally loved and accepted by him.

2 Understand that, without a revelation or biblical understanding of the horror of hell/the lake of fire and Jesus's great love for the lost, it would be difficult to be effective as witnesses to the gospel of salvation.

3 Receive a deep understanding in their spirits that *every* unrepentant person is lost for ever, and hence gain a deeper love for non-Christians.

4 Understand the life-and-death importance of obedience to God's commands to *go*!

5 Understand how to make their testimony effective as a tool in evangelism.

Key Scriptures
Read and meditate on the following Scriptures. Underline or make a note of verses that particularly speak to you.

1 *1 John 4:19–21*: We love because he first loved us. If anyone says, 'I love God,' yet hates his brother, he is a liar. For anyone who does not love his brother, whom he has seen, cannot love God, whom he has not seen. And

41

he has given us this command: Whoever loves God must also love his brother.

2 *John 3:16–18:* For God so loved the world that he gave his one and only Son, that whoever believes in him shall not perish but have eternal life. For God did not send his Son into the world to condemn the world, but to save the world through him. Whoever believes in him is not condemned, but whoever does not believe stands condemned already because he has not believed in the name of God's one and only Son.

3 *Revelation 20:1–15* (Read the whole passage in your Bible, and meditate on the following extract): Then I saw a great white throne and him who was seated on it. Earth and sky fled from his presence, and there was no place for them. And I saw the dead, great and small, standing before the throne, and books were opened. Another book was opened, which is the book of life. The dead were judged according to what they had done as recorded in the books . . . and each person was judged according to what he had done . . . If anyone's name was not found written in the book of life, he was thrown into the lake of fire (verses 11–15).

4 *Luke 19:41–4*: As he [Jesus] approached Jerusalem and saw the city, he wept over it and said, 'If you, even you, had only known on this day what would bring you peace – but now it is hidden from your eyes. The days will come upon you when your enemies will build an embankment against you and encircle you and hem you in on every side. They will dash you to the ground, you and the children within your walls. They will not leave one stone on another, because you did not recognise the time of God's coming to you.

5 *Acts 4:15–20*: So they ordered them to withdraw from the Sanhedrin and then conferred together. 'What are we going to do with these men?' they asked. 'Everybody living in Jerusalem knows they have done an outstanding miracle, and we cannot deny it. But to stop this thing from spreading any further among the people, we must warn these men to speak no longer to anyone in this name.' Then they called them in again and commanded them not to speak or teach at all in the name of Jesus. But Peter and John replied, 'Judge for yourselves whether it is right in God's sight to obey you rather than God. For we cannot help speaking about what we have seen and heard.'

6 *Matthew 28:19–20*: Therefore go and make disciples of all nations, baptising them in the name of the Father and of the Son and of the Holy Spirit, and teaching them to obey everything I have commanded you. And surely I am with you always, to the very end of the age.

Group Participation
Respond individually and as a group (as appropriate) to the following questions/prompting:

1 Our response to God's love is paramount. Do you believe you are loved and accepted by him? Discuss.

2 What is our responsibility for the unsaved, even those who are apparently in a place where they have no chance to hear the gospel (e.g. a woman in a harem in the middle of Arabia)? How do you think God feels when he has to condemn someone to hell/lake of fire when he loves the world so much that he sent his Son to die for it/us?

3 Jesus wept for the Jews whom he knew could never have eternal life so long as they rejected him as their Messiah. Why does God refuse to accept people into his kingdom who are good, law-abiding 'God-fearers', but who don't/won't accept Jesus as their personal Saviour? Why is every non-Christian, however good, kind or religious, inevitably condemned to hell by a loving and compassionate God?

4 How would you feel about weeping for someone who isn't a Christian? Have you already? If not, would you? Try to understand the cultural barrier to weeping in the Western world. Do we have the courage to confront our ingrained cultural upbringing and weep for the lost, as Jesus wept over Jerusalem? Are you able to imagine the horror of what is going to happen to non-Christians if they are not born again before they die? What does God need to do in your heart before you will have the compassion of Jesus for the lost?

5 Have you any examples of the power of love and Christian compassion in evangelism?

6 Imagine you have been told not to be a witness to the gospel in certain situations – for example, to unsaved members of your church. How can you decide between obedience to your church leaders and obedience to the Word of God? What should you do?

Prayer
Pray as a group and individually (as appropriate) the following prayers:

1 'Thank you, Lord, for your 100 per cent commitment to me. I know you love and accept me. I believe it, receive it, and enjoy your love. Amen.'

2 'Father, I know that your Word commands me to *go* and make disciples of all men. I know that you have filled me with your Spirit of love and compassion. You know that I am often disobedient. You know that I am often barren of love and compassion for non-Christians. I often let opportunities to be a witness to Jesus and what he has done slip by. I acknowledge this as a sin. Please forgive me and give me a fresh revelation of your heart for the lost. I choose to release the Spirit of love and compassion into my life in a new and stronger way. Amen.'

3 Ask the Holy Spirit to tell you to whom and where he wants you to be his witness in the coming days and weeks. Ask him to go ahead of you to prepare the hearts of those you will be speaking to about Jesus. Ask him to give you the courage and words to be an effective and faithful witness.

4 As a group, give him thanks and praise for answering your prayers.

Action

1 Talk openly with others in the group about those uncomfortable issues that you have identified. Share the good news of how love/compassion has borne fruit in evangelism.

2 Tell your neighbour (or the group if it is small enough) what you feel the Holy Spirit has told you to do, and what you are going to do after the meeting as a result.

Suggestions For Group Leaders
• Before the meeting starts on this chapter's material, review how people have got on with the actions and resolutions of last week. Ask for feedback on prayers that have been answered, and witnessing that has borne fruit.

All fruit is to be welcomed and encouraged, however weak or 'bungled' – we all learn on the job! You need to review feedback and encourage the group every week, and make sure that all group members join in building up one another. Seeing God's faithfulness, and the fruit of obedience, commitment and persistence, will build faith in everyone. If group members are so anxious about failing or being judged by their peers that they can't or won't act, the enemy will be the only one who is rejoicing!

• Steer the group through the discussion on 'the unfairness of God in not saving good people' with sensitivity and wisdom, but without compromising the truth.

There has been a steady increase in the ratio of Christians to unbelievers over the past 2,000 years. At the time of the death of the Twelve Apostles it is estimated that the ratio was 1:360. In 1900, it was about 1:27; today it is 1:7. (Facts from *Catch the Vision 2000* by Bill and Amy Stearns, Bethany House Publishers, Minnesota.)

The Church is growing and will continue to grow until God's plan for the earth has been fulfilled. The possibility of 'every nation, tribe and tongue' hearing the gospel within our lifetime is realisable! If every born-again believer would bring just one person to the Lord each year, this 'end-time' task for the Church would be accomplished in around five years!

• Love and compassion is a gift and revelation from God. You cannot do anything to generate more love in your group, but you can – if you are not careful – generate feelings of failure and condemnation, however hard you may try not to. Be sensitive to the Holy Spirit as you lead the group. Allow him to convict you and the group, and make sure every person deals with the conviction by confession, repentance and faith. Assure them of the truth. They are forgiven and their prayer for more love and compassion has been heard and answered.

Encourage the group to act as compassionate and loving witnesses in the coming week. They need to show, in word and deed, that they believe God has heard their prayer and has responded.

• Before the meeting ends, remind everyone that the next chapter is all about personal witness. They need to read the chapter during the week as normal, and then prepare (before coming to the meeting) to give a three-minute personal testimony. It will be a fun time! And no one will 'fail'. It's not a test; it's a safe time for everyone to make their mistakes in private and learn from one another. Encourage everyone to come.

If your group is large, you probably won't have time to listen to all the testimonies, and also cover the other material planned for next week's meeting. You will need to decide whether you need to split next week's meeting over two weeks. If you do, you might do everything except the testimonies during the first week, and the testimonies on the second week.

If you decide to do this, take a few minutes to explain how to give an effective 'short' testimony. You might even give some 'role playing' examples of bad testimonies and good ones. (If you've never given a testimony yourself, ask someone who *has* done this to come to the meeting to tell the group what to do.)

• Finally, be prepared to teach about hell, because there is often confusion about what it is. In the Bible, 'hell' is the English word used to translate both the New Testament Greek word *Hades* and the Old Testament Hebrew word *Sheol*, the pre-Judgment waiting place of the unsaved dead (Rev. 20:13; Ps. 6:4–5). Hell, the devil and his demons will be thrown in 'the lake of fire' to be tormented forever; the ultimate and eternal destination for all who do not receive Jesus as their personal Saviour (Rev. 20:11–15). Jesus promised that all who believe in him have eternal life; when believers die they are assured of a place in paradise with him (Luke 23:43). After the final judgment, believers will enter the New Jerusalem where Jesus and God live (Rev. 20:11–22:6).

3

THE MESSAGE

So how can you share your faith? Well, ask the Holy Spirit
to help you – remember that you and he are partners.

Reliance on the Holy Spirit

I tend to liken evangelism to using a drill to make a hole
in the wall. It's a partnership between me and the Holy
Spirit: without divine power I am ineffective and, worse,
can make more of a mess in the 'wall' than before! I
can't blast my way through to someone's heart in my
own strength, nor can the Holy Spirit do his work without
direction and the right pressure on the 'target'.

So I am always listening to the Holy Spirit's promptings,
trying to be sensitive to what choice of words (or none
at all) feel right for the moment. A good guide is the
following verse: 'Let the peace of Christ rule in your
hearts' (Col. 3:15); another translation is 'Let peace be the
umpire of your soul', which implies that you will usually
receive a clear ruling as to whether your inclinations are
from God or not!

Jesus demonstrates his reliance on the Holy Spirit
perfectly in his encounter with the Samaritan woman
at the well (John 4). His disciples were amazed that
he was talking to this Samaritan woman. They had

previously wanted to call down the fire of judgment on all Samaritans, but now God's fire of grace and love had arrived in the person of Jesus.

Jesus loved all people, but for a Jew to talk to a Samaritan was a miracle in itself. When the Jews had been conquered by the Assyrians and forced to leave Samaria, another race – the Samaritans – had been forced to settle in Samaria. They settled in so well that they adopted Judaism, claiming it was their own, with Mount Gerizim, not the temple in Jerusalem, as the holiest place. No wonder John says that the Jews had nothing to do with the Samaritans.

Jesus talks openly to the woman, asking her to do something – give him a drink of water – that would have left him vulnerable to rejection and misunderstanding. However, he presses on, refusing to answer red-herring questions about race and religion. To her amazement, Jesus reveals her life right before her eyes by saying that she has had five husbands and that the man she is now living with is not her husband. Thus Jesus turns a natural relaxed approach into a high-powered spiritual encounter.

You will learn the skills for evangelism by practice, and reliance on the Holy Spirit. Initially, you may find it hard to counter such statements as, 'The Church is full of hypocrites', 'What about those television preachers in America?', or 'The Church is only interested in money'.

Don't be tempted to defend your church or your personal beliefs; stay with the facts of Christ's death and resurrection. You may not be a theologian, but you are a witness when you testify to Jesus's divinity. He said, 'If I am lifted up, I will draw all men unto myself.'

Stay with the message. Jesus told the Samaritan woman to ask God for the living water that springs up to eternal life. Look at the result. She became a witness to her whole community. Jesus had reached beyond race, religion and politics, bringing salvation to that whole community.

How to approach people

We must start by meeting people where they are, and *then* speak about Christ. In the West, many have only heard the name of Christ as a swear word, so we have to lay a foundation of the law, the prophets, then the uniqueness of Christ and the future of humanity. The message may differ, but the principles should remain the same.

Initially, use any current topic that will lead in the direction of the gospel. When the film *Jesus of Nazareth* was shown on television, I asked people if they had seen it. Most had, so I continued. 'Did you see the crucifixion?'

People's replies will indicate their spiritual state. Usually they would say, 'Yes', and often commented on the gruesomeness of the execution, which meant that we were already speaking of Jesus!

The art of listening

Listen to people. This is one of the most vital keys to successful evangelism, both in everyday situations and in street evangelism (we will discuss this in Chapter 9).

An evangelist I knew missed the last train after a meeting and was told he would have to wait until six o'clock in the morning for the next one. He began chatting to another man in the waiting-room and they talked about general things until the man started unburdening himself to the evangelist, satisfied that he had a listener interested in his circumstances and problems.

So the evangelist listened to him for several hours, until he felt it the right time to say, 'Now, I've listened to you and I have something I'd like to say to you.' For the next two hours, he shared the gospel with him and led him to Jesus.

If you listen, you may well be rewarded by hearing someone speak, probably indirectly, of a need in their life. Everyone has a need or problem, although it may not always be obvious. These are the main needs/problems:

- The universal fear of death
- Fear of being left alone – or already alone
- Guilt
- Pride
- Severe worries/problems

If someone appears to have no specific need, simply talking about God and sharing the Scriptures is a way of producing an awareness of their need for salvation.

Dealing with the fear of death

Before I was a Christian, I believed that the world was hurtling towards complete chaos and destruction. However, hearing about the second coming of Christ led me to conversion, and that knowledge has been a wonderful anchor ever since, keeping me secure in the storms of life.

You too may meet fearful people, because where there is no hope, fear rules. They may be concerned about irreversible pollution, famine, and the threat of nuclear war. However, our gospel message produces hope. Tell people how the Bible shows that Jesus is alive and will return to rule the earth. There will be peace; his government will be first to rule with justice and love. Oppression and hunger will cease. There will be no more separation and no more tears. What a glorious hope! What liberating truth! That is the message that brought me into his kingdom.

The following are some important Scriptures for fearful people:

> You will hear of wars and rumours of wars, but see to it that you are not alarmed. Such things must happen, but the end is still to come . . . Because of the increase of wickedness, the love of most will grow cold, but he who stands firm to the end will be saved. (Matt. 24:6,12)

> [God] will wipe away every tear from their eyes. There will be no more death or mourning or crying or pain, for the old order of things has passed away. (Rev. 21:4)

Common objections to believing in Jesus

'I'm a good person – why do I need Jesus?' Whether or not people actually say this, it is one of the major objections to the gospel – one that I have met more often than any other defence. Almost all 'religious' people, whether they belong to another religion or are churchgoers without being born-again Christians, are taught to do good deeds. Even Mahatma Gandhi said, 'We can follow the teachings of Jesus, but we don't need Jesus in order to fulfil them.' Gandhi was wrong; you cannot do it alone. In fact, when I read of Gandhi's life, I saw that he too struggled with his own sinful nature.

People who adopt this position assume that their good deeds will earn them a place in heaven. Never discourage those who are trying to do good. Indeed, from Scripture we see that God will bless good deeds performed with a humble heart; in the reference to Cornelius, who was not born again, yet was 'a righteous and God-fearing man, who is respected by all the Jewish people', we learn that the centurion's prayers had reached heaven on account of his 'gifts to the poor' (Acts 10:22,31).

Knowing what is in Cornelius's heart, God sets up an angelic visitation and a divine encounter when Peter goes to his house and preaches the gospel. The Holy Spirit comes upon all who hear the message – Cornelius, his relatives and close friends – and they are baptised.

We have to be able to pray and trust that God will use the seed we have sown to convince someone of Christ's divinity. Sometimes the person is not convicted on the spot, but later, when they are at home. Of course, some people have been prepared by others, so we can go swiftly to the last part of our dialogue, when we invite them to receive Jesus. Many, however, may need to be persuaded, and we must simply continue to talk with them, gently and lovingly.

There is such a man in my church; for months he was convinced that God would accept him just as he was – he was a good person, so as far as he was concened that should be enough! Eventually he came to the point where he acknowledged that he needed Jesus, and he prayed with me to receive him.

Another encouraging example is of two women who came to the vegetarian restaurant rented by some of our church members, who had invited non-Christians to a free meal! When the two women were sitting down, I shared with everyone in the restaurant how I had come to know Jesus. Both women received Jesus and repented in tears, but one of them continued crying every day for the next few weeks.

Yet she was not crying tears of joy or repentance; her struggle was with herself, for she had believed God would accept her if she did enough good for people. Now she was confronted with the fact that she was a sinner and realised she could not reach God through this barrier. The conflict lasted several weeks, despite our efforts to help her; finally, in an evening service, she went forward to receive from God, and gloriously came to the understanding that it was 'simply Jesus, and only Jesus' who could save her and bring her to God. Since that encounter, she has brought many others to church events. This was real evidence of the value of persevering with people who trust in themselves for salvation!

With others who are already churchgoers, I will often ask questions such as, 'Did the priest explain to you what Jesus was talking about in St John's Gospel, when he said you must be born again to see the kingdom of God?' (John 3:3.) I use 'St John' deliberately, because this will be the most familiar term for those who are already churchgoers.

Anticipate the answer. They may think this Scripture is talking about infant baptism or a vague belief in reincarnation. I would then ask them politely if I can explain what it means. Most people are willing to listen, so I speak more from John 3 and add my own testimony.

Many 'religious' people feel that doing 'good works' (that is, doing good to others) is very important. They say, 'I try not to hurt anyone. I don't lie, steal or kill. I try to help others. I go to church.' Sometimes it is a bit of a shock when you tell them that the Bible says we are all sinners and have fallen short of God's standard (Rom. 3:23).

The Bible tells us that God requires perfection, which does not mean that he fires thunderbolts from heaven in disgust at our behaviour. But he does want to deal with the selfish, sinful nature inside us, because until we let him do so, even the best of us will not be fit to live eternally in God's family. This does not mean that God does not love us; it means simply that we cannot 'cure' our sinful nature on our own.

Explain that sin is not confined to crimes such as murder or being sexually promiscuous, but that it means every small selfish act or thought committed in our daily lives. I expound this point by discussing the way we all have selfish attitudes in some areas – even the person who exhibits the most goodness will have their weaknesses.

The Bible says that anyone who has broken one of God's Commandments has broken them all. Take, for example, the Commandment to have no other gods before the Lord (Exod. 20:3). Even good people may well put something that seems humanitarian and 'good' before God, such as their family; and many hold their job or house dearer than God.

This situation is illustrated in the story of the rich ruler who came to Jesus (Luke 18:18–25), asking what he had to do to inherit eternal life. He had kept the Commandments (Exod. 20) since he was a boy, so appeared sinless, until Jesus looked at his heart and discerned that he wanted to keep his money more than he wanted to follow Jesus.

In other words, he had an idol in his life, something meant more to him than God, leaving him unable to love God with all his heart, mind and strength; thus he was breaking the first and most important Commandment. This man walked away sadly from Jesus; he was still a good man, but because he had not felt able to do what Jesus asked him, he went away without the assurance of eternal life that he had sought.

Sometimes we need to explain that people's thoughts and behaviour may seem acceptable against the backdrop of our tarnished world, but when compared to the holiness, righteousness and burning purity of God, the contrasting dirt and ugliness of our thoughts and deeds can be shocking. I tell the story of a little girl walking with her mother by a field of lambs. 'Look, Mummy,' she says, 'how white the lambs are.' A week later, walking past after a snowfall, the little girl is puzzled. 'Mummy, the lambs look dirty next to the snow.'

This is an opportunity to quote Isaiah 64:6, where the prophet says, 'All of us have become like one who is unclean, and all our righteous acts are like filthy rags.'

By now, you can ask if the person you are talking to agrees with you that we are *all* sinners, before explaining that only perfect people will go to heaven. I illustrate this by telling the story of a religious person dying and then knocking at the gate of heaven and asking Peter to let him in. Peter opens the gate and tells him to wait while he looks in the Book of Life. He comes back saying that he cannot find the man's name there. The man explains that he has done his best, and has never hurt anyone.

Shutting the gate, Peter steps outside and explains that as God has high standards, only perfect people who have notched up a thousand points are allowed into heaven.

It is then that I say to the person: 'Now tell me what you have done in this life.'

'Well, I went to church every week.'

'Good, good, that's one point.'

'I helped old ladies across the road.'

'Good, that's two points.'

'I visited old people in hospital.'

'Good, that's three points.'

And so it goes on, with the highest mark at 150 points. This illustrates the futility of trusting in good deeds to get into heaven. Then I tell them, 'Supposing you invite me round for a cup of tea, and my wife knocks at the door asking for me. You wouldn't say, "I hope he's inside" or "I think he's inside". You would know for sure, and say to my wife, "Yes, he's here, I'll call him." Likewise, when you invite Jesus to live inside you, it's not a case of thinking he's there or hoping he's there. You know he's there. If I ask the question, "Are you going to heaven?", you don't need to say, "I hope so; I think so." You will know for sure. Settle it today. Make sure he is inside. Make sure you are going to heaven.'

I conclude with the reason why Jesus died and rose again, because without the Saviour of the world we could never get to heaven. I explain about the terrible sufferings of Christ, how he died in excruciating agony, his whole body wracked with the results of our sin. So great is the sin that Jesus took for us, that he cried out, 'My God, my God, why have you forsaken me?' And this came from the one who had lived a sinless life and never been separated from God. We see that there was a terrible price paid for our sin, even for good people, because we can never measure up to God's standards on our own.

I then explain how I tried to be good on my own for three years, by meditation, chanting, studying in a secret order, and developing certain psychic abilities in order to become a 'master of my own destiny'. Yet there is a limit to what we can develop when we are dead spiritually; it is our *spirit* that needs to be brought to life. 'God is spirit, and his worshippers must worship in spirit and in truth' (John 4:24).

God wants to shut down our 'sin factory'. I refer to the American Prohibition when police raids discovered crates of illegal alcohol, but could not pinpoint the liquor factory where the stuff was produced! People may find that even if they conquer one sin, such as smoking, sin breaks out elsewhere, such as in over-eating or irritability, because we still have the sinful nature we were born with. We don't have to teach babies to sin; we try to teach them to act unselfishly, by sharing their toys or obeying their parents.

People may have realised by now that they too have a love of money or even family between them and God. The Bible states that Jesus laid down his life, and those who believe and trust in him have passed from death to life.

When we take this step, God closes down the sin factory. The new 'heart of flesh' we are given often brings with it a new world-view and a desire to help humanity. This is why many of those working with the poor and refugees are Christians, seeking to love their brothers and sisters in Christ.

Everyone needs to admit that they need a Saviour who will give them that which they will never gain on their own: a new heart and a new nature through the sacrifice of Jesus alone. 'I have been crucified with Christ and I no longer live, but Christ lives in me. The life I live in the body, I live by faith in the Son of God, who loved me and gave himself for me' (Gal. 2:20).

Without a Saviour they are relying on their own deeds, which is an attitude based on pride. God tells us to turn around from our downward path to sin and death, to repent, and to accept what Jesus has done for us. The miracle of being born again takes place when we invite Jesus to come and live in us; he takes away our sinful nature and places within us a brand-new nature: 'Therefore, if anyone is in Christ, he is a new creation; the old has gone, the new has come!' (2 Cor. 5:17)

It is impossible to *work* your way to God. We will never be holy or perfect in our own strength: 'Yet to all who received him [Jesus], to those who believed in his name, he gave the right to become children of God' (John 1:12). 'Here I am! I stand at the door and knock. If anyone hears my voice and opens the door, I will come in and eat with him, and he with me' (Rev. 3:20).

The artist Holman Hunt painted a picture of Christ holding a lantern and knocking on a closed door. I ask people if they have seen this picture; many say they have. I tell them about repenting, and receiving Christ into their hearts. 'Is Jesus living in you, or is he knocking on the door of your heart, asking to come in? Will you go to heaven when you die? Are your sins forgiven?'

Most people are not sure, so I then say, 'Would you like to receive him? Shall we pray together?' After we have prayed together, the person can pray for themselves, or I sometimes lead them. Always pray for them to be filled with the Holy Spirit. At this point there is often a manifestation of power to confirm God's Word.

Then I ask, 'Where does Jesus live now?'

'In heaven,' some say.

'Yes, but where else does he live?'

'Oh, in *me*. Jesus lives in *me!*' The penny drops, understanding dawns, light shines from their eyes. 'Oh yes, Christ is in *me*.'

Roman Catholics and other church-going people

I have many Roman Catholic friends who know God and are on fire for him. Likewise, I know Anglicans, Methodists and Baptists who are on fire for God. But, sadly, there are many churchgoers who do not have a personal relationship with Jesus.

The best thing is for those who have the fire to share it with those who don't. One 'hot' Roman Catholic friend won scores of other Catholics to the Lord, but many of us will still need to go across the religious divide.

Any so-called religious person who believes that good works will get them to heaven will need a thorough presentation of Scripture. 'All of us have become like one who is unclean, and all our righteous acts are like filthy rags' (Isa. 64:6).

'I am the way and, the truth and the life. No-one comes to the Father except through me' (John 14:6). I have found using John 3:3 a wonderful tool: 'no-one can see the Kingdom of God unless he is born again'. Jesus explained this to a religious man, Nicodemus, and it is an ideal Scripture for religious people.

The question of suffering

Another common objection to the gospel is, 'How can a loving, all-powerful God allow suffering?'

Very often, people are inwardly levelling an accusation against God through this question. When training others for evangelism, I encourage them to check that they themselves no longer harbour any accusation against God in their own hearts, because they must have resolved this issue before they can answer it.

Of course, you may have a 'hiccup' day when you want to blame God for things that have gone wrong in your or others' lives, but this attitude must not be allowed to become part of your lifestyle as a believer. You need to be trusting God all the time, which is very different from the world's outlook.

In the same way, the answer to this question needs to be approached from God's standpoint, not from a humanistic stance. Start by explaining that God is just: 'Righteousness and justice are the foundation of your throne; love and faithfulness go before you' (Ps. 89:14).

'Righteous' also means 'blameless', and God has imputed that righteousness, that blamelessness, to us as believers. This means that even if we were to die tonight, in an imperfect state, we know that God will see us as being blameless thanks to Christ's sacrifice on our behalf.

Humanists

A humanist will focus on the assumption that if someone's needs are not being met, then if there is a God, he is unjust and is to be blamed. This is where *we* focus on God's character and nature. When you know somebody well, you know in which areas they can be trusted; if someone has developed to maturity in Christ, you know you can trust them in many areas.

However, God can be *totally* trusted, because he is perfect and he is love. Therefore he cannot commit any unjust action. So the problems we face on earth do not have their roots in heaven, because God is just, but have their origins on earth, in humankind.

If you make this clear, the person accusing God will find themselves confronting the nature of their creator, facing his righteousness and justice. I explain that if I am experiencing difficulties, I know that God has not engineered them for me. because he is not unjust.

In fact, blaming him would be counter-productive, as I would begin to lose my trust in the one who can actually help me – and even resolve my problem quickly, if that is according to his plan. If someone declared, 'You Christians always say it's just God's will, whatever happens', I would reply that we are not fatalists. Injustices such as slavery and racism, to name just two, have been diminished in our society, often with Christian reformers at the forefront – for example, Lord Shaftesbury in the last century. It is said that had the Church responded earlier to Hitler's ambitions, it might have changed them. The Church did not, because its understanding of the situation was fatalistic; people awoke too late and neglected to use their power as believers to change things.

I also explain that if God wanted people to obey him unquestioningly, he could have made robots. However, he gave us the power to make choices, to know him and be fulfilled in his love, or to reject him. I find it awesome that God should have allowed us to choose life or death, light or darkness, heaven or hell, and all the eternal consequences.

Even the devil cannot override our choices; if someone has made a decision for Christ and is walking to the front of a Christian meeting to affirm his choice, the devil would like to kill him if he could. He is not able to, though, because he no longer holds the keys of death and hell. He can wrestle with the person's mind, but ultimately he has no power to prevent a soul walking out of his demonic kingdom into the kingdom of Christ. What a miracle God performs each time a soul is won!

Since we have had choices since the beginning of our life on earth, I may explain to someone that it's clear that our ancestors and many nations often made the wrong choices. Historically, we can see many nations and empires that no longer exist, most recently that of the former Soviet Union.

Human beings were given the authority to govern the earth, but because of their greed and determination to exclude God from what they did, we live with the consequences of our self-willed decisions – hence the injustices, poverty and suffering in the world today.

I find that people are quite happy to discuss this subject in general terms, such as the injustices that one nation may have committed against another, or the stockpiling of food by the European Union (for example, 'butter and beef mountains') while others are dying; most will agree that the fault lies with humanity. If God were in charge of humanity's actions, that food would be distributed evenly and lives saved.

It can also be proved statistically that God has put enough food on our planet to feed all of us, but, as the Bible says, the systems of the world are corrupt: we live in an 'adulterous and sinful generation' (Mark 8:38), whose people hoard for themselves.

The Christian teacher Francis Schaeffer has pointed out that those major civilisations whose writers and artists focused on God prospered; but when they switched their focus to themselves, glorifying themselves or indulging in erotic representations of life, things worsened. This can be seen in the Roman and British empires, both of which disintegrated.

When people's minds are centred on God, however, peace begins to reign, and order is restored to human affairs. At this point I introduce, or return to, my own testimony, explaining that before I became a Christian, my life had no purpose and I seemed to go round in circles.

After becoming a Christian, God gave me purpose and, for the first time, I was going somewhere. (Sadly, some Christians are still going round in circles, mainly because of a lack of knowledge of God's character and the awareness that God has a plan for them to fulfil.)

In a later discussion you can refer to the biblical fact that humanity, given rulership over the earth, yielded that dominion to the renegade spirit, Satan, who took full advantage. Many of the evil things that happen in the world are connected to the satanic realm.

During the first discussion I usually talk about the kingdom of good and the kingdom of evil. I ask people, 'If there was someone who was full of love, wisdom, purity, power and holiness, who would do only that which was good for people, would you vote for that person to rule over you?'

Of course, most people say yes. I explain that this is the opposite to a dictatorship, which is oppressive and tyrannical, whose priority is the survival of the dictator. This concept of the kingdoms is an analogy of the kingdoms of God and of Satan. Jesus is the King who will rule with this power, authority and wisdom, who loves the people so much that he will do only what will bless them.

The dark deeds of Satan's kingdom can be witnessed in our daily news broadcasts; indeed, Jesus says in the Bible that he was 'a murderer from the beginning . . . a liar and the father of lies' (John 8:44). The Bible makes it clear that Satan set out to deceive the world and steal people away from God's love. If you look at what happens across the nations, you can perceive an invisible hand over them, causing trouble. God created the world and saw that it was good, while Satan seeks to destroy all that God made.

At this later point you can thus conclude that not only did human beings abdicate their moral responsibility for looking after the earth, but gave authority over to this renegade spirit, who may be invisible, but whose deeds are very visible. I find that few people have difficulty in grasping this fact, because many are starting to believe there is an invisible realm. This belief is helped by hearing and reading of near-death experiences and even occultic happenings.

I continue to contrast the kingdom of love and the kingdom of hatred, showing that most of the world is ruled by fear, seen at its broadest in the actions of larger nations towards smaller ones. I bring comfort by explaining that although humankind granted a renegade spirit certain authority, he has it only for a season.

In the same way, we have been given a season in which we can choose to love God and follow him with all our hearts, or love ourselves more and follow our own desires. This latter choice also gives more opportunity for the demonic renegade spirits to run riot.

Through these illustrations, you can return to the point that man has a moral responsibility for his actions, a point on which the humanist will agree. If you press this point further, you bring it to a personal level – the individual's personal responsibility for his actions. Most of us do not mind putting the world to rights, but the area of personal responsibility can make us feel uncomfortable.

When I discussed this point with my father, the atmosphere would become tense, for the Word of God cuts like a sword. So be prepared for what could be a negative or angry response, but remember that the sword cuts into the heart to make way for a seed to be planted. Later on, if you have continued to share the truth consistently, patiently and lovingly, without appearing angry or judgmental at any time, the person may well respond.

Other points to make include explaining the consequences of personal responsibility. Love allows people the freedom to go their own way; it does not control them. Thus the father lets the prodigal son go away, rather than tying him up in the attic!

Hence God will not immobilise us if our hearts are set on a wrong course of action: in fact, he has given us, the believers, the authority to prevent evil actions through prayer, but this is another topic.

Thus if a young man chooses to go out and get drunk, and then runs down a child in his car, people may ask, 'Why did God let that child die?' But God has given that young man responsibility for his life, and there will be consequences for that action.

Similarly, if someone chooses to take heroin and shorten his or her life, this is not God's action. Or if a mother is addicted to certain drugs, her child may be born with the same addiction. God permitted this mother to choose to take drugs; out of love he gives us the choice, as well as a knowledge of good and evil.

God will never force somebody to make the 'right' choices; for if you force somebody into a relationship, they will hate you. God has put the seed of truth into our hearts; we see his nature and infinite wisdom in the majesty of creation and in the death of his Son, Jesus. He also sends us, his ambassadors, to tell people of his love.

Remember to explain that God loves even those who are hostile to him; he proved this by sending Jesus to die on the cross for *all* humankind. 'And he died for all, that those who live should no longer live for themselves but for him who died for them and was raised again' (2 Cor. 5:15).

What could be more just than God becoming a man who died in order to destroy permanently the cause of our suffering? When God restores the universe to its original, intended state of perfection, there will no longer be evil in the world. But God also has a solution to the problem of evil right now; and it starts in our hearts. The big question is, 'Will you let God deal with the problem of evil in your own heart?'

However, I would not try to address the topic of suffering this fully in one sitting; I would try to be led by the Spirit of God to know which points to highlight or, indeed, to discern if the question about suffering was in fact a red herring. If the person is not interested in the answer or has put the question in order to provoke or mock, I continue with the presentation of Jesus and the cross. The key to almost every situation is to present the Messiah, who prophesied his own suffering on behalf of humankind when he said, 'But I, when I am lifted up from the earth, will draw all men to myself' (John 12:32).

Reeling in a fish

It is important to know how to lead people to God, once you have brought them to the point where they want him in control of their lives. In your discussions, you will have given your testimony (or part of it) and talked about how you have a personal relationship with God. At the right time, when you judge someone is ready to be challenged, ask a question along the lines of, 'If you could know God personally, would you be interested in knowing him?'

If the answer is yes, I explain how they can say a prayer to ask Jesus to come into their lives and take away their sin in exchange for eternal life. Then I challenge them: 'What would prevent you from receiving Jesus right now as your personal Saviour?'

Rarely do I receive a hostile answer to this question, because it is intended to challenge people who are already receptive, rather than provoke someone who is already hostile.

Assuming that the person is receptive, (even if not totally ready), then this kind of challenge will draw them out and elicit one of three responses:

1 Embarrassment.
2 Nothing/no reply. This is the time to lead them into the prayer of commitment.
3 An answer of 'No – not ready.'

So how do you respond to these various reactions?

1 Embarrassment Embarrassment is the most common response in Britain, so let the reel out a bit to give the person space. (If you are in public, they could be embarrassed about being asked to pray aloud.) I then bring out a tract I always have in my pocket called *The Bridge*, which gives a classical explanation of how Jesus became the 'bridge' between God and humankind. I ask them, 'Would you read this tonight? At the end of it, there's a prayer. Will you pray it and, next time I see you, tell me you've done it!' (If it's unlikely I'll see them again, I ask them to tell someone else that they have prayed the prayer.)

Giving people a tract with this special request has worked many times! People have returned to me the next day and told me that they prayed the prayer from the booklet the night before.

2 Nothing/no reply This usually means 'yes' to praying to receive Jesus! Ask them to pray or lead them in prayer, as they repeat the words after you. It is amazing how many people will do this.

Say a simple prayer along these lines:

Lord God, I confess that I have sinned. But now I can thank you that Jesus shed his blood and died for my sins. From now on I want to have Jesus in my life and be with him in eternity. Lord Jesus, please come into my life as my personal Saviour and forgive me all my sins. Amen.

Remember salvation is of the heart. It's not only saying words, but an encounter with God. Look for sincerity of heart and allow some who are ready to cry out themselves in prayer to God.

3 'No – not ready' Either return to talking about normal things in order to keep the friendship, or talk some more about the Lord, probing gently to see how far you can go on the subject before returning to everyday topics. Then pray that there will be another time and place for them to respond to the gospel. How you leave is particularly important; it is still part of your witness, and you are still Christ's representative.

Resist anger and never give up

Don't ever be tempted to manipulate people by hinted threats or rudeness. If you stop being friendly, you will discourage someone from listening to the next Christian who witnesses to them.

One missionary working with a previously unreached tribe was badly abused by those to whom he witnessed. He retaliated with anger, but on subsequently reading to them from the Bible about the character of a true Christian, he was shamed when they replied, 'If you can show us one of those, we will believe.' The story ended in success, for God dealt with the missionary's anger, and the tribe eventually met a true biblical Christian in him; as a result, most of the tribe became Christians.

An angry response from someone is often a good sign, because the person has been convicted of sin; thus you have, in fact, touched that person's spirit. Many angry people have responded to the gospel later and received their salvation.

Never give in to despair; remember that the Bible tells us to be ready 'in season and out of season' to share our faith (2 Tim. 4:2). God alone knows people's hearts. At certain times we will know not to cast our great truths before 'swine', but at other times, even 'out of season', we must still speak those truths.

It is not always easy to know the difference, but your key is that peace within.

Jewish people

After 2,000 years of the most horrendous persecution by Christians, it is time for us to show love to the Jewish people, both in the United Kingdom and in Israel, their God-given homeland. I would like to be able to say that it was only unsaved so-called 'Christians' who incited anti-Jewish hatred, but in fact the foundations were laid by some of the 'Church fathers' such as Jerome and Chrysostom, while the later writings of Luther provided the justification for the Holocaust. The whole subject merits our special study but is outside the remit of this book, so I shall confine myself to the following points:

1 Be sensitive to Jewish history and experience. During the Russian pogroms of the last century, priests carrying blazing crosses led the way into Jewish villages.

2 Eschew 'replacement theology', which claims that the Church has supplanted Israel in God's affections. There

are many Scriptures that contradict this false theology. However, this is the version of Christianity that many Jewish people have experienced.

3 Earn Jewish people's respect through friendship and love.

4 If you earn the opportunity to speak to them of their Messiah, take care with your words. Do not be so arrogant as to assume that a Jew will 'become a Christian'. Remember that it is *Christians* who are grafted into the Jewish root (Rom. 11:17–21), and the God of Abraham, Isaac and Jacob so loved the whole world that he allowed non-Jewish people to share in their Messiah. In this context, a 'Messianic believer' is perhaps a better term than 'Christian' to use to describe non-Jewish believers in the Jewish Messiah.

5 Remember that you should be able to present the Messiah through the *Tanakh* – what we misleadingly call the 'Old' Testament – which was the only Bible of the apostles, the first Messianic Jews. The whole move of God we see in the book of Acts was based on preaching from the *Tanakh*, so before you say, 'The Bible says . . .', be aware that a quotation from the *Tanakh* should follow.

The New Testament may be familiar to Jews from living in a Gentile culture, but while many Jews will graciously acknowledge that Jesus was a good teacher, for them it does not carry the authority of Scripture.

How many Messianic prophecies do you know? Did you know that the chances of one person fulfilling all the Messianic prophecies in the Old Testament (there are sixty-three) is about a million to one? It's a good exercise to check your knowledge of the Bible! Obvious ones about the events of Jesus's life are Daniel 9:26; Isaiah 7:14, 9:1–2, 11:2, 11:10, 35:5–6, 40:11, 42:2,

42:3, 49:7, 50:6, 53, 61:1–2; Micah 5:1–2; Psalms 16:10, 22, 41:9, 68:18, 69:8–9,12, 72:10, 110:1; Malachi 3:1 (about John the Baptist or 'Immerser'); Deuteronomy 18:15; Zechariah 9:9, 11:12–13, 12:10 (this is particularly exciting, referring to what will happen at Jesus's return). Be aware that rabbinic interpretation of certain Messianic texts, such as Daniel 9 and Isaiah 53, has changed over the centuries and they are no longer taken as 'gospel'!

6 Messianic Jews share the fundamental beliefs of Christians, but many respect the Torah, the teaching of Moses, far more than Christians do. This is a huge topic, but it is important to be aware that the Christian teaching many of us may have received about 'law and grace' has a false basis, thanks mainly to Luther's ascribing his own Catholic guilt to the Jews. (This is explained in a set of six tapes by Dwight Pryor, *Jesus, Paul and the Law*.)

How you respond to the Torah in your own life is between you and God, but be aware that Messianic Jews feel that the Church's anti-Torah theology (again, due to anti-Semitism from the Church fathers) is one of the Church's tragic flaws concerning the Jewish people. 'By our rejection of Torah, at worst we have written the Jewish people off as a people group. At best, we have confused them about God's revelation in the Scriptures. Both result in one thing – Jewish rejection of Yeshua' (*Torah Rediscovered*, by Ariel and D'vorah Berkowitz, First Fruits of Zion, 1996).

To a Messianic Jew, the teaching of Rabbi Yeshua is a brilliant commentary on the Torah, and together they provide our model for living. When St Paul (Rav Shaul) wrote that, 'All Scripture is God-breathed and is useful for teaching, rebuking, correcting and training in righteousness . . .' (2 Tim. 3:16), he was speaking of the *Tanakh*, because there was no New Testament canon at

71

that point (similar eulogies of Torah are seen in Psalm 119 and 19:1–7 among other places). Would Paul really have been referring to the Gospels and his own letters at this point? Seen from this perspective, we realise that we have no right to impose a less than perfect understanding of this aspect of Scripture on the people of the Book.

7 Understand the centrality of Israel and the Jewish people in God's purposes for human history. All your efforts will prosper when you obey God's commands to 'Pray for the peace of Jerusalem' (Ps. 122:6) and 'Comfort, comfort my people' (Isa. 40:1) – God has promised it in his Word!

Evangelist Reinhard Bonnke, who had the vision of a blood-washed Africa, relates how he was praying about Africa when God said to him, 'You pray for Israel and I'll give you Africa.'

As history seems to be speeding up and prophecy is fulfilled (including the exodus of Jewish people from the former Soviet Union), it is vital that we understand our part in God's plan for us regarding his purposes. With anti-Semitic persecution increasing in the former Soviet Union, has your church thought of practical ways to bless the Jewish people, such as sponsoring a coach to bring them home to Israel at just $80 a head? People engaged in this work report that Russian Jews are amazed to find Christian volunteers helping them. How exciting to help fulfil prophecy!

What Muslims need to hear

Muslim theology is based on the belief that good works can get you to heaven, but Muslims are never sure when they have done enough to have earned their ticket.

Therefore a Muslim needs to hear that Christ is unique,

that he is the only Saviour of the world who died to pay the price for our sin, and that God made it happen out of love for us. Use Scriptures to support what you say.

Muslims are also intrigued by the revelation that God speaks to ordinary people. In their thinking, God only speaks to the holy men – like the prophet Mohammed. Therefore, if God speaks to you, you must be holy. They often ask me, 'What did he say?'

Many Muslims are open to hearing about Christ; you will soon realise who is open and who is closed, after a few conversations. Islam is a religion of the mind, not the heart. There are many rules and hard codes of behaviour. As you speak of your Lord with Muslims, see your efforts as planting, sowing or watering. If you do not give up, eventually you will reap.

When Iraq lost the Gulf War, Muslims became very open to the gospel and many Iraqis became Christians, while the Kuwaitis became harder to reach. God has a timetable. The harvest will be reaped. Every nation, every tongue, will be represented in heaven. Hallelujah!

Buddhists

Although Buddhists believe in 'the divine inside every human being', they will burn paper money and offer things to their ancestors, among many other practices, in order to atone for their sin and earn approval. Explain about man's sinfulness as you would to a so-called religious person.

Hindus

I have found that Hindus respond positively to my ravings about the character and nature of God! Sometimes I ask them, 'What is your god like?' Because they have millions of impersonal gods, it is difficult for them to specify. Then I ask, 'May I tell you what my God is like?' Almost always, the answer is yes.

I tell of his love, how he is alive, that he desires a relationship with people, stressing that the personal love of God is paramount, because this is totally the opposite of what they have experienced – an impersonal idol made of stone or wood. There is no point in condemning Hindus' own religious practices, though, for the reasons we have already discussed. You must be Christ-centred, always returning to the good news that salvation is for everyone.

Give them your own testimony in three minutes or longer, if appropriate.

Teenagers and young people

The vast majority of young people have never heard the truth about Christ's love; at school, many will have been exposed only to comparative religious studies. Many only know Christ's name as a swear word. While there are adults in this category too, they still appear to have a greater understanding of the gospel. If basic knowledge of Christianity were measured on a scale of zero to ten, I would be staggered by the number of young people on zero.

Rushing in with the good news without first building some degree of trust is pointless – youngsters will simply reject your message. It is better to talk about hobbies, such as music or football, for interests build friendship. Share your faith later when they are much more likely to listen. Keep listening to the Holy Spirit – and know when he is telling you to stop!

Once when I was talking to three teenagers, the most vociferous one had to catch a bus. The other two became much more open and lively after his departure, and we talked to the point where I felt I could challenge them: 'Have you ever asked God to reveal himself to you?'

They hadn't, so I suggested they said this prayer before they went to sleep that night: 'God, if you're there, will you reveal yourself to me?' I asked them, 'Will you take this challenge?' 'Yes,' they replied.

I was so encouraged by their response that I wanted to continue telling them about Jesus, but they had started to lose concentration and I sensed that the Holy Spirit was indicating that he had finished.

Building relationships with teenagers takes time. Although most of them act 'cool' and exude a detached attitude, usually they are open to (and sometimes inwardly desperate for) attention and love. Their outward appearances can sometimes be a real turn-off, so I generally ignore what I see. In many instances, the outward appearance of hardness crumbles as you continue to relate to them. My own nephew, who was busy projecting this hard image, has now changed and is looking for truth and love. It took some time to get there, but I believe that if we keep the door of our lives open to young people, eventually some will come through it.

Having been a rebel myself when younger, let me encourage you to continue to pray and love teenagers. After conversion, I discovered that people had been praying for me. Others reached out and came and shared the message of eternal truth with a hostile, angry young man. Only God knows the end result of our witness.

Love is always the key to the heart of a person, whatever label may be on the outside.

Happy fishing!

SUMMARY

• Think about your non-Christian friends and acquaintances. How can you share the gospel with them?

• Keep practising writing and speaking your own three-minute testimony.

FOR GROUP DISCUSSION

Aim of the Chapter
By the end of the meeting, participants will have:

1 An understanding of the importance of depending on the Holy Spirit in witnessing.

2 An understanding of how to, and how not to, witness.

3 Prepared themselves to deal with some typical 'objections' to the gospel message.

4 Thought about helpful approaches to different 'people groups'.

5 Given their testimony (briefly!) to others in the group.

Key Scriptures
Read John 4:1–26, the woman at the well. Identify lessons from it concerning:

1 How Jesus used the woman's questions to lead her to the point where she could receive the truth of who Jesus was and to believe this truth.

2 How the woman tried to oppose and challenge the gospel that Jesus was telling her, and how Jesus 'countered' her objections.

3 What you think finally got through to the woman and convinced her to receive and believe the truth.

Group Participation
Respond individually and as a group (as appropriate) to the following questions/prompting:

76

1 Every person is unique. Different aspects of the gospel will touch the hearts of different people. How can we know what emphasis to give for the gospel to bear fruit?

2 Have you ever encountered the objections to the gospel message given in this chapter? How should/could you deal with them? What are the most common objections you have actually encountered, if different to these? How did/should you deal with them?

Prayer
Jesus had an open heart of love for those who rejected him as well as for his disciples. It cost him his life. Talk about the need for open hearts in evangelism and the costliness of having an open heart. Pray as a group and individually (as appropriate) the following prayer:

Dearest Lord Jesus. Thank you for taking away my hard heart of stone and giving me a soft heart of flesh when I accepted Jesus. I want to walk in the truth of what you have done more and more. I want an open, loving and sacrificial heart towards the lost. I know that nothing is impossible for you, and that you have heard my prayer and answered it. Where I have been hard-hearted towards others, please forgive me because I have been unwilling to pay the price for loving others as Jesus did. Please give me opportunities this week to show my newly opened heart. Thank you. Amen.

Now pray in pairs for individuals you know who need more of your love, for a fresh and stronger outpouring of God's love and compassion in the churches in your area, and for opportunities to be a witness to those who raise various objections or red herrings when they hear the gospel.

Action

Before coming to the meeting, every group member needs to think about his testimony, jot down a few items to talk about, using the structure given in this chapter, and have a *timed* practice at home. (Don't try to memorise your testimony, as an actor memorises his lines. It needs to be spontaneous and open to the leading of the Holy Spirit to be effective.)

At the meeting, each group member should give a three-minute testimony. Other members of the group should say what they liked most about the testimony. (Remember, if the group is too large, postpone the testimonies until next week, but use this time to show the group how to prepare and give a powerful testimony.)

Suggestions for Group Leaders

• This session requires more teaching by you, or directed discussion, to achieve its aims. Think how you will handle the meeting beforehand. Prepare notes if necessary. Think through how you want to lead the discussion times. Remember to keep discussions focused on the topic and frequently summarise the key points made. Only pursue red herrings when the Holy Spirit says you must!

• Make conscious decisions about when to get the whole group to participate, and when it is better to break up into smaller sub-groups, or even pairs of people. Remember that it is easier to control the flow of the whole group, but that it takes much longer to let everyone have their say.

• When the time comes to give testimonies, make sure that everyone has a go. Watch especially that the timid ones don't manage to avoid this important opportunity to overcome their self-consciousness and fears and to learn to become more effective in ministry. Try to pair like with like – the more talkative and extrovert together, and the quieter and more introverted together – to lessen the

78

chances of the shy ones being squeezed out by the bold ones! Check that you are obeyed when you say it is time to start and stop speaking. Stress that the comments that are invited about each testimony *must be encouraging.* *Criticism is banned* – however justified or 'constructive' the criticiser may feel the criticism is.

4

DIVINE APPOINTMENTS

Almost every failure in the Christian life can be traced to a prayer failure. The same is true when you *succeed* in a Christian endeavour: it's because you or someone else prayed. It has been said, 'A little prayer brings little results; much prayer produces great results.'

It is the disciplined excitement of prayer that launches us into successful witnessing. Billy Graham was once invited to conduct crusades in a certain country. 'How long have you prayed for these crusades?' he asked. 'One year? Pray for another year. Then come and invite me again.' When asked what was the most important part of preparation for his campaigns, he said, 'Prayer, prayer, and more prayer.'

A wonderful story is told of a massive banquet. The Lord himself was there to present a trophy to the person who had started a very large church in a certain city. Thousands were gathered. The senior pastor and associates of this church were there. Everyone was waiting for the Lord to call the senior pastor; but instead, the Lord rose and called out the name of a woman whom nobody knew. The people were shocked and surprised to learn that she had started that church in her prayer room.

The church in that area was born through one intercessor who continued in prayer until God raised up this large church. The Lord says to those who pray in secret that he will reward them publicly. This woman, like many other thousands of intercessors, will be rewarded openly when that day comes.

Never expect others to do your praying. You need to pray about every aspect of your witness: ask God to show you who to speak to, when to speak to them, and what to say to them.

The sower and the seed

In the parable of the sower, the Word of God is represented as seed that a farmer went out to sow. The state of the ground represents the human heart. Do you remember the times when you weren't ready to hear the gospel? The devil snatched the word away before it could embed itself in your heart and bear fruit. Or perhaps you thought about it for a while, and then the cares of the world dislodged the seed? When did you finally believe the gospel? The answer is, when your heart was ready. If someone appears hard and unreceptive, then break up the ground in prayer. I usually pray, 'Lord, give them a spirit of wisdom and revelation so they can understand the truth. We bind the devil from preventing their leaving his kingdom to listen to the truth.' So the first thing we do is speak the truth to people, but we prepare their hearts by prayer.

Perhaps you could assess the progress of each person you witness to on a graph graded from 1 to 10. Your listener may not yet be ready for immediate salvation; if this is the case, do not despair. Speak the words that the Holy Spirit gives you and slowly bring the listener further along the graph. I often pray, 'Lord, give me a divine appointment with someone on 9.75!'

81

Where is your prayer focus?

'I'm believing in God for a new car, a new job and a godly wife.' I often hear Christians telling each other that they are 'using their faith' to believe that God will provide things for them. Some also 'believe for' an improved prayer life and quality of Christian life, but this is all inward-looking. The Christian life is *not* an end in itself, any more than going to a gym to develop muscles is an end in itself.

'But seek first his kingdom and his righteousness, and all these things will be given to you as well' (Matt. 6:33). When believers seek God's will for them in obeying the great commission, they will receive the things they need as a resource for God's work.

The first apostles did not focus their spiritual energy on themselves or their circumstances; they looked outward, constantly desiring that God would open doors for them to spread the good news of the Messiah. In other words, they were believing that he would give them divine appointments.

A divine set-up

A divine appointment is an occasion when God sets up a situation or an opportunity for us to speak about Christ or lead a person or people to Christ; to see healing or deliverance take place or to receive provision for a need. It often results in people's spiritual needs being met in ways that are beyond our wildest dreams.

Try recalling your own salvation. Whom did God bring into your life at that time? Many of us were truly 'set up' by God. He brought three women some 20,000 miles to witness to me. If he can do that for me and similar miracles for you, why should we imagine that it is difficult for him to set up divine appointments in our own witness to others?

Faith for winning the lost

Most people don't think in terms of divine appointments; they just let life roll by. There are also many who work hard at witnessing, but bear little or no fruit. Like all of us when we do anything in our own strength, they achieve little, as if they were trying to drill that hole in the wall without the power switched on, as we discussed in Chapter 3.

Why not start believing that God will provide opportunities to spread your faith? I long to hear people say, 'I'm believing God for three divine appointments this week.' Most people would have a 100 per cent improvement if they started believing God would provide just *one* divine appointment a week!

Divine appointments are not automatic; God will provide them when we ask for them. We have to be ready, through regular prayer and the building up of our inner being by reading and meditating on God's Word.

I promise that if you pray regularly and make a conscious decision that, 'No matter what it takes, I'm going to obey his promptings', you will become sensitive enough to the Holy Spirit to hear when God tells you to go. Don't expect an audible voice; divine appointments often come from fleeting thoughts, impressions or hunches.

How to hear God

Many Christians who ask me for advice tell me that they cannot, and do not, hear God speak. Yet most of them will tell me, in graphic detail, what the devil has been telling them. Surely, when Jesus – and not the devil – is our Lord, this is a contradiction!

God loves to communicate with people. He would walk and talk with his first created man and woman – Adam and Eve – every evening. When that closeness was lost, God still continued to speak, either in an audible voice or through his prophets.

Now God has spoken to the people on earth through his very own Son, Jesus. When Jesus died and rose again, he removed the barriers that came with the disobedience of Adam. Now the Holy Spirit, God himself, was able to come and live in humanity, restoring God's loving relationship with his children. The Holy Spirit of God speaks to us, counsels us and leads us into all truth. Communication lines are always open. Jesus said, 'I know my sheep and my sheep know me' (John 10:14, see also John 10:27).

Are you one of the Lord's sheep? If so, then you *do* hear his voice. If you say that God never speaks to you, then how did you become a born-again Christian? God *did* speak to you. God always speaks, but we do not always recognise his voice. He speaks in a diversity of ways, mainly through his Word, the Bible.

It is normal to hear the voice of God! Our main barrier to hearing God is stark unbelief. Repent and stop confessing the lie: 'I can't hear God's voice.' Tell God you are surrendering your will to his will, then the channels of communication will be opened.

'And without faith it is impossible to please God, because anyone who comes to him must believe that he exists and that he rewards those who earnestly seek him' (Heb. 11:6). You believe he exists, so pick up the phone and call! He always honours his Word. I prayed for a sound-proof flat to pray in – God obliged with walls of nine-inch brick! He loves faith, and will pass over thousands of casual inquirers to get to the diligent one whom he says he will reward.

He invites you, 'Call unto me and I will answer you and show you great and mighty things you do not know.' You do not have to wait until you get to heaven in order to get your reward! And one of your rewards will be to hear his voice, the still, small voice of the Holy Spirit. He speaks to our human spirit by thoughts that come into our mind.

'Call to me and I will answer you and tell you great and unsearchable things you do not know' (Jer. 33:3). He does not say that he *might*, but that he *will*. God has promised that he is 'near to all who call on him' (Ps. 145:18). In other words, unlike earthly telephone lines, his lines are never engaged!

One day, the President of Korea telephoned Pastor Yonggi Cho, but his secretary refused to disturb him to speak to the President. When the President's wife phoned Yonggi Cho later and suggested he should sack his secretary, Pastor Cho explained that he had been involved in a very important meeting. He had been talking to the heavenly President.

The battle for the mind

Have you ever had an argument going on in your mind? At a time when you wanted to witness to someone, have you had the thought that they wouldn't want to hear, that you'd be wasting your time and, worse, that the person would think badly of you? Have you doubted that you hear from God directly?

These thoughts are certainly not from God, so learn to put a stop to them by bringing them 'captive to Christ' (2 Cor. 10:5). There are three voices competing for your attention: the voices of self (the flesh), the demons, and the voice of Almighty God himself through the Holy Spirit, which I can best characterise as a loving insistence.

You can stop the voices of self and the devil through prayer and faith. You can submit to God, resist the devil and he will flee from you as in terror (Jas. 4:7). Rebuke him and command him not to speak. Jesus sternly told demons, 'Be quiet! . . . Come out of him!' (Mark 1:25; Luke 4:35.)

As one of Jesus's disciples, you have the same authority to dispense with demons (Luke 9:1). Only then can God's Holy Spirit and the angels speak to you. Why not stop right now and pray the prayer of command? Pray out loud, 'I command every argument to stop! I command every proud imagination that exalts itself against the knowledge of God to be cast down. I now bring every thought captive to Christ in Jesus's name.'

Once you're tuned in, you will appreciate how creation often shouts of God's existence, revealing his majesty and omnipotence through the splendour and intricate beauty of nature. God used to communicate with me through nature a great deal: trees bending in the wind had a message relevant to my situation. That was a certain season; now he speaks more clearly to me, in a still, small voice.

Time in God's presence

Jesus's relationship with his Father was always his priority. However busy he was, he would make time for prayer: 'Very early in the morning, while it was still dark, Jesus got up, left the house and went off to a solitary place, where he prayed' (Mark 1:35). I once woke up early in the morning with a prompting to pray and, after several hours, found I had the answer to some problems that had puzzled me for some time.

Jesus was always on time for his divine appointments because he had such a close relationship with his Father. 'I tell you the truth, the Son can do nothing by himself; he can do only what he sees his Father doing, because whatever the Father does the Son also does' (John 5:19).

The story of Jesus meeting with the woman at the well (John 4:4–26) was a divine appointment, as was the occasion in the following chapter (John 5:1–15), when Jesus was sent to heal just one man out of many at the pool. He knew which one was ready to be healed because he was in tune with his Father.

As Jesus spent time with his Father, so he was strengthened by him and enabled to continue his ministry. Spending time with the Lord should be a time of feasting on his love; it reminds me of David's reference in Psalm 23:5: 'You prepare a table before me in the presence of my enemies. You anoint my head with oil; my cup overflows.'

When Moses had spent forty days with the Lord on Mount Sinai, his face was radiant – he had no choice about being on fire for the Lord! And as we draw near to Jesus we will receive so much of his life that it will overflow from us to others. It is that overflow of godliness – divine love, joy, peace – that meets people's needs. Without those fruits of the Spirit I am operating in my own flesh, and I am largely ineffective.

A man once had a vision from the Lord of a very skinny, sickly looking being and the Lord told him, 'This is your spirit man, your inner man.' He was amazed to see how weak and anaemic his own spiritual condition was. It was because of his poor condition that he did not see any fruit in his life. He was fearful, often sick and defeated. The Lord told him, 'Feed on my Word. Spend time with me. Build up your spirit man.' For the next seven to eight months, the man prayed, read the Bible, and constantly meditated on the Scriptures. Soon he began to receive invitations to preach. Signs and wonders followed his ministry and there was salvation, healing and deliverance. All of this came from the overflow of being with Jesus.

The Lord is the instigator of our appointments, but, like Jesus, we need to hear what he is saying and be obedient to his directions. It is good to take time over our daily reading and studying of the Bible, to be unhurried and attentive to God's voice, expecting him to speak to us. You will find it helpful to have a notebook and pen handy when you are waiting on God, to jot down what he says to you, together with a Scripture reference. Satan will try to twist or snatch away God's Word from us, so it is helpful to be able to look back and then state categorically, '*God* said . . . !'

Grace to believe the impossible

'For it is by grace you have been saved, through faith – and this not from yourselves, it is the gift of God – not by works, so that no-one can boast' (Eph. 2:8–9). Grace is the divine ability God gives us to repent and be saved. We receive that grace through faith, which is another gift from God: we call it 'saving faith'. Now since there are many millions of people alive today, surely you will be able to believe that God can give grace to someone among them for salvation? *We* cannot make this happen, but when we exercise faith and confidence in God, he does the impossible for us and makes it happen.

Whenever we become conscious that God has set up a divine appointment during our normal daily business, we need to obey in spite of any risks involved – or fear of man! Fear of the Lord should always override fear of man. When we are actively seeking to be a blessing to others, God can and will use us.

He also demonstrated that his promptings do not always

make sense to our natural reasoning, as I discovered on one particularly grey day in my geriatric unit at the hospital where I worked as a young Christian.

An almost perceptible cloud of gloom hung over the hospital that day and the needs of the patients seemed to be particularly draining, so I was a grateful man when I slouched from the ward for a coffee break. On the way to the canteen, an unbelievable thought came into my mind: 'Go and talk to Mr Fisher about me.'

Mr Fisher had been a patient on our admission ward. He was very confused and had been placed in a long-stay ward. 'Lord,' I reasoned, 'he can't understand a word I say.' I had already tried many times before to tell Mr Fisher about God.

However, the feeling persisted and grew even stronger, so I visited Mr Fisher and spoke with him of Christ's love for about twenty minutes. Much to my amazement, he was completely rational and we had a wonderful conversation! He was overjoyed to accept Christ as his Saviour. After we had prayed the prayer of salvation together, he returned to his confused state, which he maintained until the day he died.

God knows when and how things work. I know that Mr Fisher went to heaven. It was a great success for the kingdom of God despite the fact that it had been a pressurised day and I was not exactly feeling on top of the world. Yet I could have shrugged off the promptings from the Lord with thoughts like, 'Mr Fisher can't understand. Forget it!'

I have also found out what happens when you operate with the best intentions, but *outside* of God's will. In Malaysia, during a very successful ministry trip in 1979, I was invited to lead some meetings. I felt a reluctance in my spirit about accepting, but thought that I could not pass up such a great opportunity. So I accepted the invitation and accordingly prayed, fasted and worked hard at making those meetings a success. But to no avail! It was simply not God's will.

Divine appointments in Acts

Both in the Bible and today, many such meetings come about as a result of prayer or reading the Word of God. Ananias was told, 'Go to the house of Judas . . . and ask for a man from Tarsus named Saul, for he is praying. In a vision he has seen a man named Ananias come and place his hands on him to restore his sight' (Acts 9:11–12).

Philip was sent to the Ethiopian eunuch as he was reading from the prophet Isaiah (Acts 8:26–38). Simon Peter was praying when he received God's call to meet with Cornelius, described as 'devout and God-fearing; he gave generously to those in need and prayed to God regularly' (Acts 10:2). The angel of God tells Cornelius that his prayers and gifts to the poor had come up as a memorial offering before God (Acts 10:4).

Cornelius was not yet a believer but was waiting for salvation. God often sends us to those like Cornelius who are seeking understanding and praying for an answer so that they can respond to him.

Divine appointments with leaders

I believe that the Lord wants us to ask him for opportunities to speak to those in authority and lead them to Christ.

I have a friend from India who is always praying that he will be used to speak to kings, rulers and those in authority. While in Malaysia, coverage of his meetings appeared in the newspapers, which is remarkable as the Malaysian government is Islamic. Because of the reported miracles, the Muslim king summoned him to the palace to pray for a close relative, who was instantly healed. The king and all in the court then invited the evangelist to preach.

Many hours later he tried to excuse himself, declaring that he had a meeting to attend and must not be late. However, the king pressed him to stay on, promising to fly him to his meeting in the royal jet. Here was a remarkable divine appointment, the result of believing prayer!

Many reports were later circulated that the king had received Jesus as his personal Saviour. We will not know, as the king died three weeks later. It was also reported that he was poisoned because of his faith in Christ.

In Acts 8, Philip met the Ethiopian, 'a eunuch of great authority', who was wonderfully converted. As a result, Christianity spread throughout his land. You do not always know to whom you are talking when you speak about Jesus. Many Africans or people from developing nations who are here in the United Kingdom may be rulers over hundreds or thousands of people in their own lands. The former President of Zambia, Kenneth Kaunda, came to study here. It is reported that he once asked for a drink of water only to be spat at! How history might have been changed if he had met a Christian here who had shown him love and led him to Christ! Have you prayed and asked God to lead you specifically to those who are leaders? Start praying today; God himself will open up such opportunities. It is his will. If a slip of a girl can be responsible for witnessing to Yonggi Cho, then God can use us with the influential, the wealthy and potential leaders.

Love never fails and never gives up. If we are willing to pay the price, to pray, to obey the voice of the Lord and love people, we will have many divine appointments. Are you ready for yours?

SUMMARY

Divine appointments may be the result of:
• Prayer: Acts 9:10–19, 'He is praying'; Acts 10:1–23,
'. . . and prayed to God regularly'.
• Bible reading: Acts 8:26–38!, '. . . heard the man
reading Isaiah the prophet'.
• Relationship with God: Mark 5:16–20: John 5:1–9,
where Jesus knew which man to go to at the pool.
• Normal daily activity: John 3:1–21, where Jesus was
willing to give up his sleep; John 4:5–26, where speaking
to the woman was more fulfilling than food.

FOR GROUP DISCUSSION

Aim of the Chapter
By the end of the meeting, participants will:

1 Have more faith in, and a better understanding of, the
role of divine appointments in effective witnessing.

2 Be more committed to their daily time of prayer, Bible
reading and listening to God, and understand better the
importance of spending time with God in their personal
growth and ministries.

3 Have discovered that most biblical examples of divine
appointments are linked to prayer.

Key Scriptures
Read and meditate on the following Scriptures. Underline
or make a note of verses that particularly speak to you.
*Acts 9:10–19, Acts 10:1–23, Mark 1:35–8, Acts 8:26–38,
John 5:1–9, John 3:1–21, John 4:5–26.*

Group Participation
Respond individually and as a group (as appropriate) to
the following questions/prompting:

1 As you read these Scriptures, note the importance of 'divine appointments' in Jesus's ministry and the growth of the early Church. What do you think would have been the consequences, if the person given the 'divine appointment' had failed to respond to the leading of the Holy Spirit?

2 Have you had any 'divine appointments'? How did you feel about responding, and what were the fruits of your obedience and faith? Briefly tell the group about them.

3 What are your experiences – problems and blessings – of your personal daily 'quiet time' with God? If you aren't currently spending time with God like this, what is stopping you? If you are, what can you learn and do as a result of this chapter/session that will help your 'inner person' to grow strong and fruitful?

Prayer
Pray as a group and individually (as appropriate) the following prayers:

1 Ask God to give you divine appointments in the coming week. Stand in faith for the answer to this prayer. Thank him in advance for answering it. (Many believers are taught to use their faith to believe God for *things* – money, jobs, etc. What a privilege it is to be able to believe him for *people* – new converts and disciples!)

2 Confess those things that are preventing you from being an effective 'divine appointee'. Ask God to show you what you should do to become more effective, and to give you the right words to say with boldness and conviction.

3 Thank him in advance for the divine appointments and enabling he has already released into your life and for the fruit you *will* bear in the coming week.

Action

As a group, share your thoughts on these points:

1 The understanding gained this week about 'divine appointments'.

2 What changes are planned to improve on hearing God's voice.

3 The ways in which you can build up your 'inner person'.

Suggestions for Group Leaders

• If some group members are not 'baptised in the Spirit' it may be hard for them to hear God's voice, and therefore to recognise 'divine appointments'. They may, therefore, feel uncomfortable in the meeting as others reveal how God has spoken to them in the past. In their embarrassment they may respond a little aggressively. Be sensitive. They are being convicted by the Holy Spirit and prompted to receive his 'filling to overflowing'.

Don't be embarrassed to talk about this important anointing. Give anyone in the group (who wants it) the opportunity to be baptised in the Spirit. (If you aren't confident that you can or should talk about and lead people into baptism in the Spirit, invite someone to the meeting whom you know is able to do this.)

Teach as effectively as possible to prepare the ground; a good study book is *The Holy Spirit and You* by Dennis and Rita Bennett (Kingsway, 1990).

Remember that the enemy has a vested interest in preventing believers being filled to overflowing with the Holy Spirit. He knows his kingdom will suffer a major setback when the awesome power of the Holy Spirit is released in yet another believer! Don't let him intimidate you or any member of the group!

• Many Christians feel awkward at the suggestion that

they need to hear God's voice. They don't think they can, even though they know the Bible says that Jesus's sheep hear his voice. Their problem is usually *not* that they don't hear his voice, but that they don't recognise it as his voice. Almost all Christians do hear God's still, small voice on a regular basis. Many don't realise he is speaking to them. They think it is just their own thoughts, or even the enemy's lies! Remember, if they couldn't hear God's voice, they wouldn't be born-again Christians. Only the Holy Spirit can bring us to repentance and faith.

5

ON HOME GROUND

Are you looking for a great ministry? Do you have a roof over your head, a place to live, a place to sleep? If the answer is yes, then you have a marvellous opportunity for a great ministry! Look around and see what you have to hand, just as God encouraged Moses to use his staff, the only piece of equipment he had with him.

Much of Jesus's ministry was conducted in various homes, often over the meal table. Read the Gospels. Life bursts through the pages as salvation, miracles, healing, discipleship, prayer and friendships flow out of Jesus's friends' homes. What a wealth of blessing we miss when we confine ministry to the church building!

Whole family ministry

Before all the male readers switch off, let me assure you that hospitality is not a women-only ministry. It is really a ministry for the whole family, and I'm talking about far more than dinner for six on Wednesday. One of the key aspects of our ministry has been availability, which has meant our home has been an extension of our hearts: if you have an open heart, you will have an open home. That has often meant being available at all hours, which has necessitated my being there; after all, what man would be happy about his wife opening the door at 2 o'clock in the morning?

Children can also be involved, simply by being themselves! If you keep the right balance and give your children enough love and time, they too will grow up understanding that a home is God's gift and should be shared with those in need of a family or salvation (usually it's both!).

True hospitality

A wounded soul is not crying out for matching tea cups; someone who is lonely or in pain is looking for love, even over a plate of baked beans. So please don't be deterred from issuing invitations to people if you are single or only have a bedsit. The root words of hospitality are 'hospice' and 'hospital', with their overtones of healing; in the same way, we would like to see all believers' homes as places where Jesus lives 'to bind up the broken-hearted' (Isa. 61:1). A substitute word for 'hospitable' is 'welcoming'; if you are hospitable and people feel at home in your house, flat or room, you will win many for Christ. You know this for yourself: the places you like to visit are those where you feel welcomed and accepted. When I was a new Christian, I would go to a Christian friend's home just to feel the peace there. This was probably the reason that Jesus often went to Bethany to be with Martha, Mary and Lazarus. (You can walk to Bethany from the Mount of Olives, where Jesus taught.) He went to their home because he was always welcome and would be refreshed with sleep, food and friendship.

The Bible urges us to give hospitality (Rom. 12:13). I am convinced that when all believers of all persuasions open their homes to the lost and to each other, we will have a revival.

Learning from another culture

Having married an Asian girl, I was fascinated by the tremendous hospitality of the culture in West Malaysia. People arrive, often without any notice, and stay overnight – sometimes this may mean sleeping on the floor! They act just like one of the family. It is part of the culture to be polite and loving – above all, your guests must leave full and happy, otherwise the visit is deemed a failure. This gives us some insight into the acute embarrassment felt by the hosts when wine ran out at the wedding feast in Cana (John 2:1–11). No wonder Mary asked her son for help in this embarrassing situation! Perhaps that is part of the reason why Jesus changed the water into wine.

I soon saw that hospitality is a great strength in Asia; even those with limited resources practise fine hospitality. The Asian Christians make use of every occasion to present the gospel in their homes: birthday parties, anniversaries, Christmas parties and special celebrations – all are the forum for exciting testimonies and fine preaching, which result in others becoming Christians. When we returned to our own home in England, we decided it would be an Asian home with an open door and no rigid diary! Perhaps I adapted too quickly to Asian hospitality in an English climate for Joyce, because I happily brought people home without notice at any time! Joyce is a great cook and quickly devised ways of coping with providing dinner for six when she had been expecting one, but she admits she was challenged at first by the demands of this unpredictable ministry. Her solution is to cook for an army, which means there is food for an army of guests or for several days!

When she was feeling stretched or tired, revelation for her came from the Word of God: 'Offer hospitality to one another without grumbling' (1 Pet. 4:9). She explains:

'I realised that we are commanded not to grumble; it is a direct order from God, so I had to learn not to complain. I had to accept that God had brought them for some special reason and, after all, I wanted to be part of God's work.'

In England, Joyce noticed that the expression 'An Englishman's home is his castle' is frequently true! But among believers we cannot afford to have this attitude. If Jesus was standing there, would you pull up the drawbridge? He promises a special inheritance for those who open their hearts and homes to the needy, his family, because, 'I tell you the truth, whatever you did for one of the least of these brothers of mine, you did for me' (Matt. 25:40).

Joyce realised that it is very easy to be influenced by the world's way of 'entertaining', which is not always the same activity as offering hospitality. When she first came to England, she saw that for some women, entertaining meant displaying their best crockery and finest possessions. But when she and I were working for YWAM and living in one room, she sensed that God was speaking to her about hospitality: 'I argued that we only had a few cups, some of them cracked, and nowhere to cook, but God told me I should begin with what I had, cracked cups and all, and he would supply whatever else I needed once we began . . .'

So we realised that we could at least ask someone in for a cup of tea. Some really uplifting times followed, with lots of fun and friendships formed. Having only one room to entertain in is a real test of who your real friends are, too!

My wife and I have agreed that our home should be used by God for his purposes. We determined to have more rooms than we needed, and to trust the Lord to provide the money for a bigger house and for the extra food, heat, etc. that would be used.

This is, in many ways, a costly ministry, but it has produced many disciples in different parts of the world. Think like God thinks; he is a big God. Small thinking will not help your home resemble the kingdom of God, because without faith it is impossible to please him.

Why not take up a faith challenge and turn your life and your house over to God's use? Pray that God's kingdom will come, and for his will to be done in your home. God says he is able to do exceedingly abundantly more than we ask or imagine by his power at work within us. That power of the Holy Spirit is at work in you right now. Be renewed in your thinking; God will provide as you reach out in love to the lost and broken people around you.

Open all hours

As you get involved with people, God will call on you to use your resources for his purposes. This has happened to us many times, even during the night. In 1982, St Mark's Church in Kennington had linked with YWAM and the Bethany Fellowship for a parish outreach. One hundred 'YWAMers' had been talking to people on their doorsteps. Colin Urquhart came to preach, and we saw about ten people wanting to become Christians every night for ten days.

One of these people was Robert. Robert and his friend had stopped and listened to the gospel of God's love, then arrived at the evening service, where they had opened their hearts and accepted Jesus Christ as Saviour and Lord. But what happened next *could* have meant the loss of one of our new souls.

Early one morning – at 2 a.m. – I awoke, aware that the bell had been ringing for some time. Trying to focus my sleepy eyes in the darkness, I seemed to take an age to leave my cosy bed. I found Robert standing on the doorstep, clutching a suitcase and crying. He looked nervous and ready to dart off like a sparrow at the slightest sign of rejection. Fortunately, I was too sleepy to register any emotion as Robert spoke: 'It's me mum. She's thrown me out,' he said. I looked more closely at him, waking up fast as I felt God's love for him growing within me. Reaching out my hand, I drew him in: 'Let's go and have a cup of tea.' His eyes were brimming with tears as we made our way upstairs to the kitchen. Joyce and I showed Robert around the spacious flat that we rented. 'Please make yourself at home and help yourself from the fridge. This is your room.'

Afterwards, when he was alone in his room, we heard Robert crying. Later he told us how welcome and loved he had felt when told it was his home. How crucial it was for the Lord to have an open door through which to receive one of his beloved children!

A bricklayer, Robert had once been involved in a gang fight where a young man had died. He told of his involvement in violence, drugs and immorality. It was amazing to see this man, now placid and open, thinking deeply and asking many sincere and searching questions. He was earnest to meet God. He had enthusiastically told his family what had happened. His mother, a Roman Catholic, had misunderstood him, thinking that he had betrayed the faith and become a Protestant. The tension and arguments increased until she had thrown him out.

Robert was an intelligent, quick-witted man, thoughtful, polite and full of gratitude. He now has his own flat and runs his own business. He visits his mother almost every week and they get on very well.

Of course I could have given Robert £10 and said, 'I'm sorry to hear that. I'll take you to the nearest hostel.' Certainly, that would have been better than doing nothing, but he had been led to Christ because we had a policy of open hearts and an open home.

Does that mean we take in anyone off the street? No, that would be foolish. However, if you are led by the Spirit of God, you will recognise God's guests: 'Do not forget to entertain strangers, for by so doing some people have entertained angels without knowing it' (Heb. 13:2).

Long-term guests

Robert was not the first or the last guest to stay longer than a month in our Asian-style home. Over the years we have usually had at least one person in our guest room for several months of the year. In the St Mark's ministry in particular, I found myself looking after new believers at home as well as at work.

Although discipling was usually the last thing I wanted to do after a full day of ministry, I saw greater fruit in the lives of our guests than in any other area of ministry I tackled. People who lived with us for three to six months would be discipled in our home and then return to their own churches, often overseas, as much more mature believers.

Salvation over supper

In the Middle East, the cultural setting of the Bible, Jesus and his followers also used the gift of hospitality to present the gospel. In the West, we would do well to learn from the pattern of the Master's ministry. The ever-practical Bible teaches us to invite into our homes the blind, the lame, and those who cannot repay with money or by opening their own home to us in return.

The advantage of inviting people home is that you can befriend and win the trust of people who would never immediately accept an invitation to church. Be careful not to preach at them immediately, though, or you might never see them again! Yet neither should you compromise your own way of life as a believer; if you do, your guest is unlikely to see a great difference in your lifestyle and outlook to those of the world.

We have found that the Holy Spirit makes a way for us to share our faith without any fuss, simply by answering people's questions. At one time, we had Dorothy, a Chinese Buddhist girl from Malaysia, staying with us while she attended a course. We were living as part of a community with three other people staying with us, and we were all living by faith. Every morning we met together to pray and would present our petitions to the Lord as a family, especially if there was a bill to pay! This girl witnessed these sessions and also the way we prayed before meals. At our very first meal together, she asked why we did this, and Joyce was able to explain that we were blessing God for providing the food.

Simply living with us all from day to day showed this girl that our faith was real. She was present at many conversations when we discussed how God had spoken to us, and every time she would ask questions: 'Why do you do this?' 'Why do you pray like that?' It was particularly exciting for Joyce, who spent the most time with her at home, to experience someone gradually opening up to the gospel.

Then one Sunday morning I was preaching in church and ten people responded to the invitation to receive Christ. I was very moved to see that Dorothy was one of them. Although we had been told that Dorothy was a hard person to convert, staunch in her faith in Buddha, here she was now, following Christ. She was still full of questions, so Joyce spent time with her and helped her with her difficulties. One of the things that had affected Dorothy was the way God had miraculously provided finances for us. Later, when she returned home, we received glowing letters of her growth. In Singapore, Dorothy did some discipleship training with YWAM, and than went on to its University of the Nations in Hawaii.

One man arrived from West Malaysia with marital problems. We knew his wife very well; she was a Christian studying over here, although she had slipped further and further away from her faith. Now she had found someone else and her husband was distraught. He had travelled here to be reconciled with her, but she had refused. The first night that he stayed with us, he tried to cut his wrists. We lovingly talked to him saying, 'We will help you, but don't do that, it solves nothing.' As he was a staunch Hindu, we kept our talk about Christianity low-key, hoping our lives would witness to him. One day, I gave him a Bible and said, 'Read this story book.' After that, I often noticed his light on at two or three o'clock in the morning. He was reading his story book! In his own testimony he said, 'That was a funny story book. It speaks, and it spoke to my heart!'

We never forced him to come to church, but one day he came of his own accord and responded to the altar call that I gave. He stayed with us as a new Christian for six months. His marriage was not saved, but he was.

During those six months he was full of questions. Again, Joyce did most of the discipling. He is now a Christian businessman and owns his own restaurant. He has remarried, has children, and is a respected leader in his home church. What a change Christ made in him!

One key to coping with strangers in your home is to relax and get on with your lives serving the Lord. I can't pretend that Joyce and I never disagree, but if you wait until your relationships and your decor are perfect and your children are beautifully behaved, your ministry will never get beyond the front door! After all, if you are concerned about what people think of you, your root emotion is pride, rather than love for others.

So let people see you as real people, sincere in your relationship with the living God, even if you struggle at times. They will be more impressed by your sincerity and hope as you pick yourselves up and continue, than if you paste on 'evangelical smiles' and pretend your life is one big success story. And if you never sinned in your own home, how would your guests have the opportunity to see your reliance on God's grace?

The first house churches

Homes were often used for fellowship and church meetings in New Testament times, and Jesus accepted the hospitality and food offered to him by individuals and families. These were, perhaps, some of the more fruitful times of his ministry as he shared his life with both friends and enemies in a more intimate way than out in the open air.

For centuries, the Jewish people had celebrated the Lord's feasts in their homes, with food at the centre (Leviticus 23 is a helpful summary), and after the death of the Messiah, new believers continued to meet in the most natural way for them – over meals in each other's homes (Acts 2).

After the sacking of Jerusalem and destruction of the Second Temple by the Romans in AD 70, it was no longer possible to meet in the temple courts as well. What with growing opposition from the religious hierarchy in the diaspora (a prayer designed to weed out 'heretics' was introduced to the synagogue services which believers would have found impossible to speak), private homes were the only place in which adherents to the rapidly growing Messianic movement could freely worship and teach the Word.

Creative ideas for the home

To those who say they do not have the time to use their homes for evangelism, my answer is, 'Be creative!'

Think how you can include a non-Christian when you eat – we all need to eat! Just throw in some extra food for one more. Or have a coffee break with a non-Christian neighbour. Invite non-Christians into your home and include them when you watch television or videos as a family. Turn 'the big game' or the 'big event' into an opportunity for friendship evangelism. If you have a non-Christian partner who would oppose this ministry, ask around in church and find out who has an open home and then go and help them.

I have one particular idea about bringing a foreign student into our home: we will only accept a non-Christian! Many come to England for language courses each year, why not offer yourselves as hosts?

On one occasion God spoke to me about befriending people who come to the United Kingdom from developing countries. I shared this in our church, St Mark's, Kennington. The key point the Lord made was that such people are very open to hearing the gospel during their first year here. Their own cultures are generous in hospitality and their close-knit families protect them from the harsher side of life, so they often yearn for friendship while in this country. Sadly, they often find that they are subjected to racial prejudice, abuse, and even attacks. After a year or two of this, they tend to toughen up in order to survive. Their hearts become hardened as a result.

Offering love and hospitality to these people can be very rewarding. I encouraged all our people at St Mark's to welcome overseas students into their homes. The YMCA was run by Christians from our church at that time, and we had splendid opportunities to share our love, food and homes. It worked beautifully, especially with those who had just arrived in the United Kingdom.

Cheer up, it's Christmas!

Christmas is a key time for hospitality, especially because so many suicides take place at this time. The attempted suicide rate in one part of the United Kingdom tripled over the Christmas period. Each December, we ask God what he wants us to do. Often we have been directed to visit family and relatives, while at other times we have sensed we should open our home to those who have no family and would be lonely over this period. But be prepared for spiritual battles if members of your wider family are not Christians – I have spent more time in spiritual warfare over what was supposed to be my holiday than during many working weeks!

One year we invited Ahmed, based at the YMCA in Stockwell, for Christmas Day, along with ten others, predominantly Asians. What a day it was – Asians certainly know how to party! There was lots of super food, laughter and games.

Ahmed was a political refugee from the Lebanon. He had had to flee for his life but, as his wife refused to come with him, he had left her and the children behind with the house and business. As a Muslim believer, he told me that the relationship had finished because she had not obeyed him.

That day, I began to witness to Ahmed, but he resisted. I sensed the Lord was saying to me, 'Be quiet. Don't say anything.' So I stopped speaking of Christ and allowed Ahmed to enjoy the family atmosphere. Later, he went to church and was converted in a remarkable way. Christmas was the first time that he had felt at home in the United Kingdom since arriving from the Lebanon.

Today, Ahmed loves and follows Christ. When his wife heard he had become a Christian, she considered him dead and received a divorce from the Muslim clergy. As you read this book, please stop and pray for Ahmed as things have not been easy for him. Ask God to bless him with a job and to use him as a witness among other Muslims.

If you sense you should host people without families, be wise and invite a mixture of Christians and non-Christians, or you will find yourself outnumbered when it comes to choosing music and television programmes. A good sprinkling of believers ensures that you will not have to sit through hours of unsuitable entertainment.

The cost of creativity

'Now the tax collectors and "sinners" were all gathering round to hear him' (Luke 15:1). If you do not want your possessions spoilt, then you will need to think about the cost first. Our team had to clean out the bugs after some tribal people left our home in the Philippines. Pots and pans somehow got the non-stick covering scraped off, and carpets were covered in children's food.

In the Philippines we rented the bottom part of a house and it was always full. Small children peered in the windows at first light and came for food. We made the mistake (or was it?) of feeding them on our first day, and they came *every* day after that! Mothers and babies came at ten o'clock in the morning, and the young people packed into the house every evening. It was a fun time, though, and many became Christians, and others who had drifted away from their beliefs were restored to faith. 'A few days later, when Jesus again entered Capernaum, the people heard that he had come home. So many gathered that there was no room left, not even outside the door, and he preached the word to them' (Mark 2:1–2).

At home with miracles

'And these signs will accompany those who believe: In my name they will drive out demons; they will speak in new tongues; they will pick up snakes with their hands; and when they drink deadly poison, it will not hurt them at all; they will place their hands on sick people, and they will get well' (Mark 16:17–18).

Opening up your home to Jesus will release a flow of the miraculous. Why was Lazarus raised from the dead, when many others died and were not revived? My experience tells me that opening up hearts and homes always results in God's blessing. Jesus knew Lazarus (the Bible actually states that Jesus loved him) and his sisters, and because they knew him intimately, they were able to get a message to him immediately in a crisis.

The second chapter of the book of Mark gives us a marvellous account of how Jesus used someone's home, but I wonder how prepared the home-owner was for the miracle (and mess) that followed? Try to picture the following scene in your mind.

A big crowd had gathered at the house. News about miracles quickly spreads everywhere. Jesus was big news and people were talking about him throughout Israel. When the crowd had gathered, he did not start with friendly, polite, low-key evangelism. The Bible states, 'He preached to them.' This was a sermon he never finished, at least in the traditional sense of the word, for he, the Master, was interrupted. Remember, the house was filled not only with friends, but also with sinners and teachers of the law of Moses – those whom people would have respected as learned Bible scholars.

This gross interruption of the Master's sermon was because some 'nutters' were digging through the roof, right into the main room. (What would your reaction have been? It may indicate where your heart is!) But the Bible says, 'Jesus saw their faith.' He did not see the gaping hole, the unseemly mess; instead he saw their faith, and that indicates where his heart was!

Jesus, of course, responded to their faith; he will always respond to faith. How did Jesus see their faith? By their actions. In this case, the digging through the roof and the lowering down of the paralysed man. They just knew that if they got the paralysed man to Jesus, he would be healed. Jesus knew they believed by their actions. They could have said, 'The house is full. The Master is busy and we will catch him just as he leaves, at about midnight.' No, they were not timid. They were bold, determined and full of faith. Yet they were not rebuked; instead, they were commended for their faith.

Of course, I am not suggesting a 'roof-destroying ministry' – although the Bible says that everything that is not of faith is sin! (Rom. 14:23.) Who repaired the roof? We do not know. All we know is that the once-paralysed man walked home, his sins forgiven, and no one seemed to care about the roof. There can be a cost to evangelism, but the blessings and rewards far outweigh that.

So don't just eat and talk with your guests – pray for the sick and for one another. Joyce's uncle in West Malaysia began a prayer group with just three people. After a year, though, it had increased to 200! There were conversions and healings every week. He had a big house, but it does not matter what size home we have – we can use what we have. You will witness miracles if you really believe that Jesus wants to save and heal in *your* home.

Prepare with prayer

Prayer must be the starting point of using your home for God. However, beware of two extremes: not using your home at all, or using it so much that the needs of the people swamp the whole household and cause unnecessary stress.

Tell God that you want to open up your home, and ask him who it is he wants you to have in your home. Pray with your partner, listening to each other's prayers as each one is prompted by the Holy Spirit; you may discover your partner has more creative ideas than you had expected!

One of the most welcoming things you can do for a guest is to pray for them before they arrive. You know yourself that you feel warmly disposed towards someone whom you later discover has prayed for you, and you may have been surprised to experience an unexpected degree of friendliness from someone for whom you have prayed. So we always ask the Lord what he wants us to do for each guest and how we can bless them. Sometimes he gives us Scriptures to pass on to them; it has really excited us, particularly Joyce, to see how certain Scriptures have encouraged people.

Use discernment

If your partner is a Christian, ensure you have prayed together and are in agreement over the choice of guests. Frequently I would arrive home unexpectedly with lots of people. Joyce always did marvellously in catering for them, but the Lord was about to teach me a lesson! I found out that a Russian prince who attended one of our services, received prayer and claimed to have been healed of cancer, had nowhere to live, so I brought him home to stay.

Joyce is a very godly woman and often receives words of wisdom from the Lord. In the early days of our marriage I did not always listen to her – to our cost!

On this occasion, Joyce said, 'I don't feel right about him. Something is wrong. He shouldn't be here!' 'No, no,' I argued, 'God loves him; so must we.'

For the next three months our home was oppressive and my wife looked strained. The man turned out to be impossible. One day, in prayer, the Lord told me to ask him to leave. Our guest was a master in manipulation and made me feel wretched, but as soon as he was gone the oppression lifted. We later found out that he was a con-man – someone who specialised in conning Christians!

When you allow God to use your home, listen to what he is saying. There is a huge difference between being selfish and being genuinely tired and open to oppression. This is a great ministry; protect it. My wife and I have needed, at times, to draw back; to slow the pace, or even stop our ministry of hospitality to 'mend nets'. It would be foolish to go on fishing when your nets have holes in them! We have allowed the Lord time to adjust, heal and build sweetness back into our relationship. There have been times when people have come to our house and only found a lukewarm welcome, because we were out of sorts. But we have endeavoured to repent and use our home to the best of our ability. His grace, love and power do the rest.

May God bless your home as you choose to use it to win the lonely and the lost to Christ.

SUMMARY

• The New Testament Church met in people's homes (Acts 2:46; Rom. 16:3–5, 23; Philemon 1:2).
• Jesus often ate, taught and ministered in homes (Luke 10:38, 19:5).
• Commands about hospitality (Rom. 12:13; 1 Pet. 4:9; 3 John 5–8).

- Be in agreement (Amos 3:3).
- Be ready to preach (Mark 2:2).
- Count the cost (Mark 2:4).
- Expect supernatural signs (Mark 2:12).
- Be prepared for persecution (Mark 2:6).
- Make a decision *today* to use your home. Decide to invite a non-Christian (or non-Christians) to your home (be wise about the opposite sex).
- Pray now; be open to opportunities God is sending your way. He will help you to love and win someone to Christ. And don't forget to take time to 'mend your nets'.

FOR GROUP DISCUSSION

Aim of the Chapter
By the end of the meeting, participants will:

1 Have a better understanding of the importance of their homes as places where non-Christians can meet Jesus – alive, well, loving and active – in the 1990s.

2 Have an opportunity to decide to commit their homes to the service of their Lord.

3 Know that the root of all hospitality is love – with or without all the trimmings.

Key Scriptures
Read and meditate on the following Scriptures. Underline or make a note of verses that particularly speak to you.

1 *Acts 2:46, 47:* Every day they continued to meet together in the temple courts. They broke bread in their homes and ate together with glad and sincere hearts, praising God and enjoying the favour of all the people. And the Lord added to their number daily those who were being saved.

2 *Acts 18:2–3:* There he [Paul] met a Jew named Aquila, a native of Pontus, who had recently come from Italy with his wife Priscilla . . . and he went to see them . . . he stayed and worked with them.

3 *Romans 16:3–5:* Greet Priscilla and Aquila, my fellow-workers in Christ Jesus. They risked their lives for me . . . Greet also the church that meets at their house.

4 *Philemon 1:2:* . . . to Apphia our sister, to Archippus our fellow-soldier and to the church that meets in your home.

5 *Luke 10:38:* As Jesus and his disciples were on their way, he came to a village where a woman named Martha opened her home to him.

6 *Luke 19:5–6:* When Jesus reached the spot, he looked up and said to him, 'Zacchaeus, come down immediately. I must stay at your house today.' So he came down at once and welcomed him gladly.

7 *Romans 12:10–13:* Be devoted to one another in brotherly love. Honour one another above yourselves. Never be lacking in zeal, but keep your spiritual fervour, serving the Lord. Be joyful in hope, patient in affliction, faithful in prayer. Share with God's people who are in need. Practise hospitality.

8 *1 Peter 4:9:* Offer hospitality to one another without grumbling.

9 *3 John 5–8:* Dear friend, you are faithful in what you are doing for the brothers, even though they are strangers to you. They have told the church about your love. You will do well to send them on their way in a manner worthy of God. It was for the sake of the Name that they went out, receiving no help from the pagans. We ought therefore to show hospitality to such men so that we may work together for the truth.

10 *Hebrews 13:2*: Do not forget to entertain strangers, for by so doing some people have entertained angels without knowing it.

Group Participation
Respond individually and as a group (as appropriate) to the following questions/prompting:

1 Which stories in the chapter moved you especially? How did they touch you?

2 Do you have any testimonies of God moving because you/others were willing and able to open your/their home(s) to him?

3 What do you think is the personal cost of opening your home in the ways described? What, if anything, is stopping you from using your home in the ways described both in this book and in the Bible?

4 Do you think all Christians are called to be hospitable to others, or only those with a special anointing to do so? Are you open to give hospitality in your own home/room?

Prayer
Pray as a group and individually (as appropriate) the following prayers:

1 Thank God for those Christians whom he has called to open their hearts and homes to others in sacrificial love. Ask him to protect them – physically, emotionally and spiritually – and to strengthen them.

2 Pray against all obstacles – human, physical and spiritual – to the anointing for hospitality being released and practised in the Church. Pray that God will so prosper his children that they will be able to afford homes large enough to entertain strangers, fellow workers and even angels.

115

3 Earnestly pray this prayer, if you can pray it from your heart and want to see it answered:

Father, thank you for opening your heart and home – heaven – to me.
Please anoint me and my home to receive others. Forgive me for those times when I have turned away those you sent to find hospitality under my roof. Please send someone to me who needs my hospitality, home and love. Thank you, Amen.

Action

1 Each group member should tell his neighbour (or tell the whole group if it is small) what he is going to do to overcome obstacles to him being used to offer (even more) hospitality to non-Christians.

2 Decide to invite a non-Christian (or non-Christians) to your home during the coming week (be wise about inviting the opposite sex!) – even if it is only for a cup of tea. group whom you believe it is right for you to invite, or why you feel it is right not to invite someone.

Suggestions for Group Leaders

• As you know, it is hard for Europeans (especially the English?) to open their homes to others, even those they know quite well. This is a spiritual problem, as well as a cultural problem. Expect group members to react in some way to the subject covered in this session – some with embarrassment, some in self-defence, some under conviction from God, and some under condemnation from the enemy. You will need to steer the meeting sensitively, and make sure that it retains a positive and Christ-centred focus.

• Remember that conviction is from God. Whenever we

116

confess our sins and ask him to forgive us, he does – immediately and completely. When we repent and do what he wants, we are again restored to a position of perfect peace. Condemnation is from the enemy. Satan will lie and say, 'You are useless and always will be. There's no hope for you. No wonder God can't use you. He won't even love you unless you pull up your socks. And, in this particular area, you are so useless that you don't stand a chance of improving.'

• Be especially sensitive to those who have non-Christian or 'difficult' spouses or children/teenagers. Acknowledge the very real problems they may face in opening their homes to others. If this applies to anyone in the group, encourage that person to link up with another group member, or a Christian friend, whom they can help to offer hospitality in their home. The person receiving the help in their home will welcome such support and encouragement – giving hospitality is hard work at times! It will also enable the person with the 'difficult' home environment to get out and about.

• Tell the group they will have the opportunity at next week's meeting to speak about what happened when they fulfilled their intentions of offering hospitality.

6

BE CREATIVE

Our God is a creative God. The very first chapter of the Bible tells of his creativity, and as we look around us we can see the infinite variety of his creation: majestic, ever-changing clouds and sunsets, tiny creatures, the different shapes of leaves and trees. In the same way, he made human beings to be unique, with no two exactly alike.

Now consider the diverse ways in which people that you know came to believe in Christ and you will find that no two were exactly the same. That's why we need to be in tune with God if we are to take full advantage of every opportunity; in other words, we must think creatively, just like God does.

Creative evangelism should start with prayer – reaching out to our creative God who has an infinite number of ideas, and always knows the appropriate method for the time, place and person. Take time to wait on God, listening to what the Holy Spirit is saying; it's unfailingly exciting to walk with God in this way. When did you last let him know you were ready for an adventure in evangelism?

Creative evangelism also involves looking at what you have at hand. For example, as we have already discussed, you have a home, whether it is a palace or a tiny room; most people have relatives and friends; you may have a telephone, a car, a job. There are opportunities to witness for Jesus at bus stops, stations, shops, garages, hospitals, old people's homes, sports centres, on trains, planes and at parties. The list is endless. You can use birthday cards, Christmas cards, answer machines, tracts, leaflets, books and posters. Sometimes we can be asking God what to do, while he may in fact be telling us to use what is at hand.

Tracts

I choose my tracts very carefully – after all, they are representing the King. I have to admit that I detest the presentation of some tracts. Any tract you hand out should be short, not wordy, but clearly illustrated so that people can scan it quickly and get a seed of the truth in their hearts. Please don't use scruffy, inferior material. If it is bent or dog-eared, throw it away.

I like tracts because they help us witness, but I warn people against hiding behind them; there is no substitute for a believer sharing their faith, their personal account of meeting their Saviour.

Booklets

For those who are more interested, a single Gospel account proves a good tool. Some will take a Gospel home and read it through, whereas the thought of reading the whole Bible instantly sets them up for failure.

Books

It's not difficult to find out who is a bookworm and who struggles to read any sort of book; just ask some probing questions. Try not to give books to those who will not read them.

I will feed a bookworm with several up-to-date testimonies about the power and love of God, prayerfully trying to relate the choice of testimonies to their need. I have recommended some testimonies at the back of this book (see Resources List).

Have you had a turn-out of Christian books at home recently? For some time, cutbacks have forced libraries to function on shoestring budgets, which has meant that librarians are usually grateful to receive gifts of books. Libraries contain plenty of books on the occult and witchcraft, but the religious books they do have are frequently unhelpful. If necessary, reason with a librarian for a fair representation of Christianity – I have done this, and my books have never been refused. You might also want to give Christian worship cassettes to your library, or the gospel on cassette for the talking-book section.

In one church, we asked the librarian to come to church to receive a cheque to buy new Christian books, which resulted in her becoming a Christian, and her assistant, someone who had drifted away from her faith, returning to Christ.

Films and videos

Because we live in a visual age, in which most people get their information from the television, I often give or lend videos. Mostly I sit with the viewers to watch the video, so that we can talk about it afterwards.

For those people who already have some interest in Christianity, I use *Viva Christo Rey*, a film about a group of middle-class Christians in Mexico who sold their second cars to feed the down-and-outs who lived on a rubbish tip, 98 per cent of whom had tuberculosis.

It was documented later that through both prayer and medication, tuberculosis had been eradicated in the area.

Ian McCormack's video testimony of being raised from the dead after experiencing hell is also excellent (See Resources List at end). Useful films to break people's mind-sets are *Chariots of Fire*, *The Hiding Place*, and *The Cross and the Switchblade* (a bit dated now, but still relevant).

The *Jesus* film, based on Luke's Gospel, has been recorded in over a hundred languages and has won more people to Christ than any other gospel tool. It is great for mission; we have seen hundreds become Christians as a result of it. Recently we showed it in the former 'killing fields' of Uganda. In this rural area, no one had ever seen a film, let alone a film about Jesus. Whole villages flocked to watch and hundreds responded. What a tool for the gospel! You could minister with this film alone in unreached places.

The six-hour videos of Franco Zeffirelli's *Jesus of Nazareth* have also proved an eye-opener to some, especially the crucifixion scene.

Witnessing at work

As a new Christian I really went over the top witnessing in my workplace, and you may not want to follow me in this! I tell people, though, that an evangelist is meant to get out of the trench and go over the top, while the others are meant to follow him. I preached to everyone who moved! I had my own system – everyone must hear the gospel at least once. The senior nursing officer, the charge nurse, the ward sister, the nurses and the patients all had to hear – and they did!

About twenty nurses responded to the Lord at that time – all of whom had been influenced mainly by a

Christian woman working in administration. She was the one who took me to church when I was converted. Can you picture twenty new Christians sharing their faith all over the hospital? It was a glorious time!

Each week, I would bathe the geriatric patients by winching them down into the water on the ambulift. While they washed themselves or I washed them, I shared the gospel, and a number asked me to pray with them to receive Christ before they died.

Some flatly refused to hear about the gospel, of course. One new patient, who was bathed and preached to, was asked by the sister if he wanted to go to the service the following day. He said, 'No, thank you, sister. I've just had a service in the bathroom!'

Be honourable with the way you use your work time; no one should be an evangelist on the boss's payroll. Apart from my bathroom preaching (I was working at the same time!), I confined my evangelising to the coffee breaks and after work. I would believe that God was going to give me those opportunities to speak to the right people and made myself available, with the result that I often sat and talked with patients after work.

We once carried a young male nurse to church. He was very sick but, after Pastor Robin Rees had prayed for him, he walked out of church by himself. In the hospital, a Buddhist, a Sikh, and non-believers came to Christ, while Christians who had drifted away returned to him. We used to hold prayer meetings that were a bit noisy and went on a bit late, but we were 'babes in Christ' and did not know any different!

Predictably some persecution arose in the form of mockery and rumours that sex orgies were going on! The hospital was a very dark, oppressive place, and the fact that God could move there was a remarkable testimony to his grace and power.

Yet the people who mocked me the most threw a big

party when I left. They bought gifts and shed some tears, for in the end they were sad to see me go! I realised at the time that, even though they mocked me, deep inside they respected what I was doing.

Keep fired up and praying, and do not give up on your workmates. Do your best to live a godly life before them, and do nothing that might jeopardise your integrity. The Bible stresses the importance of an upright character and disciplined habits, such as timekeeping and quality of work.

Non-Christians are not morally blind – they know how a Christian should behave. A homosexual ward orderly with whom I worked and shared the gospel said that he realised that I was genuine and that he had seen a real change in me (he knew me before I became a Christian). He then mentioned another man we both worked with, a Christian who had drifted away from his faith, saying that he considered him a phoney. Non-Christians perceive more than we realise.

Leisure-time opportunities

Old friends Do you remember those people you met on holiday? You promised to swap photos and keep in touch, but didn't. Or the people you used to work with, or those old neighbours and school friends? If you telephoned or visited these people, they would be curious to know what you were doing now, which provides a wonderful opportunity to give your testimony and share the gospel. Pray first, of course. I pray for one old friend every time I pass his house. At the right time, I shall visit him.

Telephone skills Telephones are an exciting tool. 'Oh, sorry, wrong number' can be answered with, 'No, God bless you. You didn't get the wrong number. Jesus loves you, and so do I!' Take a few minutes to share the gospel with the caller.

One evangelist tells the story of going to an area where no live church was in existence, so he used the telephone directory and went from A to Z. He rang people and said, 'Jesus loves you. Can I take a few minutes and tell you about him?' The response was mixed. Some said no, but others said yes. Those who were Christians were just delighted to hear another Christian voice. A church was formed before the evangelist left that town – all through using the telephone. And when you pay your telephone bills, put a tract inside. But make sure it is not a red bill!

Buses and trains Standing at the bus stop or on a railway station can be a place of grumbling or a mission field, depending on how you look at it! The people have nowhere to go, the bus or train is twenty minutes late, and you have that time to share the good news with your neighbour.

One day, while on a train journey with my wife, I felt I should share the gospel with her. Joyce caught on quickly. While I spoke about the Lord, a man sitting opposite us was on the edge of his seat, hanging on to every word. What joy when I led Joyce in the sinner's prayer! He heard it all, responded, and then his stop came.

Cars and planes Cars can be a tremendous place of witness. At sixty/seventy miles an hour, you have a captive audience – they can hardly get out! A friend of ours has a Mercedes and often brings hitch-hikers to church. The ashtray or cassette rack can become a tract rack.

One of the best places to share the good news is on a plane. Pray that you will be sitting next to those who are open to hearing about Christ. Imagine sixteen hours with a budding evangelist! We have certainly had some fun!

Shops Going shopping or getting petrol? God is not an economist. When I pray about where to go, God often directs me to the smaller shops and to local petrol stations. The butcher laughs and calls me 'the vic'. Questions are asked and answered: 'What do you do?' 'Oh, let me tell you.'

We have had hours of 'seed-sowing' in shops. A Muslim family we met in their shop attended our home group, where the back condition the owner had suffered from for twenty years was totally healed. In his excitement, he shared this news with friends, including other Muslims at the local mosque. Sadly, they persecuted him. We enjoyed having his family for meals – he was certainly the only Muslim shopkeeper in the area selling Christian books and videos!

We still do the bulk of our shopping at the supermarket, but we buy some things locally. It is a bit difficult to build a relationship in the big places, which are more like a conveyor belt. 'Next!' 'Smile, Jesus loves you!' And then you are gone!

Restaurants Restaurants can be fun. Say grace aloud; it will guarantee some response. We were once with a wonderful Nigerian bishop. He often used the lift and the taxi in which to witness. It was a treat to be with a 'professional'. We took him to the best restaurant, as we thought a bishop deserved the best. He was in his flowing robes, an outstanding character, full of wit and charm.

During the meal the proprietor came over and spoke to us. Then, after the meal was finished, he asked the bishop to have coffee with him. They talked for an hour and a half, during which time he opened his heart and troubled life to the bishop, who took him through the Bible. What a privilege to see the gospel in action in everyday life!

Hospitals Hospitals are still a tremendous place to witness. Often when visiting a church member or a friend there, I get talking to the person in the next bed. Once, when Joyce had an overnight stay in hospital, she was reading her Bible when someone questioned her about it. By the time I came to visit her, she had led three women to Christ and they had lined up for prayer to be healed!

Old people's homes There are many people in old people's homes who are very lonely because they have no one to visit them. Those in charge will not usually turn down a request to visit the lonely. When you visit your own relatives there, reach out to the others in the home. Do not be afraid to talk about Christ. Many old people went to church in their younger days.

Has your church thought about visiting an old people's home as a team? Most old people love hymns, so sing some traditional hymns and get them to sing along with you. Share your testimony with them and preach.

When I was a new Christian in my first church, the church team took me to an old people's home and to the hospital each month to help develop my preaching. When I preached, some of them yelled out, and others got up to go to the toilet! It was sometimes very noisy, but I just carried on. The remarkable thing was that our church team led many to Christ in one-to-one conversations after these services.

The potential is unlimited. I can see prisons, hospitals, schools and old people's homes being evangelised with people's creative, God-given talents.

'Bring and Share' We once started a 'Bring and Share' in church on Sunday afternoons, in which musicians and creative people met to 'jam'.

They brought their friends into this relaxed setting and it was really exciting to see Christians and others use their God-given gifts to present the gospel. Some sang or played instruments; others recited poetry. Drama, dance, testimony, a short sermon – all have been employed, and the response has been amazing. It is up to a leader to find out beforehand what people propose to contribute, and ask others to share brief testimonies, ending up with a short talk if appropriate.

Sports centres Have you tried to use a sports centre as a place to talk about Jesus? Tony, a bodybuilder, has the most outlandish Christian tee-shirt that I have ever seen! When he goes to train at the sports centre, he answers the questions about his tee-shirt. He is fit, strong and built like a truck. What better person to share the gospel with another 'hulk'? Sports centres of all kinds, or swimming pools, are excellent places to share the gospel.

Waiting rooms Another excellent place to witness personally is a dentist's waiting room. All the better if you have a baby with you – either for attracting admiration or making a noise; they're real ice breakers! The same goes for dogs; try walking in the same place at the same time every day and see who else is out walking.

The Open Door charity shop

It is very rewarding to find what godly, creative ideas can do. Mandy, a young single mother, told me a while ago, 'I never would have gone to church. Some friends had tried to talk to me about religion and I just wasn't interested. If it wasn't for the Open Door, I would not have come to the Lord.'

The Open Door charity shop was a creative idea that God used in a mighty way. Based in Central Square, Wembley, north London, the shop acted as a bridge between the street and the church.

'Why don't you open a shop on the High Street?' Robin Rees had asked one day. I said I would pray about it, thinking, 'As if I haven't enough to do.' I quickly managed to dismiss this negative thought. By this time, I was an associate pastor of a fast-growing church and, yes, my duties did keep me busy, but the idea of a charity shop would not go away. In fact, it grew stronger and stronger, and I began to realise that God was in it.

Suddenly a unit right in the heart of Wembley's shopping area became available. In same ways, it seemed a crazy, idea – the kind of project none of us, except Robin, had had any experience of. 'If it is of God, God will have to provide!' said the senior pastor. Our church budget was already stretched. 'OK, Robin, Let's go for it!' I said.

As Robin proceeded with the plans, the company that had originally agreed to us using the premises changed its mind and refused. Anyone who knows Robin Rees will tell you of his tenacity. He certainly wasn't prepared to take no for an answer. He telephoned again; the reply was, 'No way.' So we prayed, and eventually the company gave in and said yes.

That was our first miracle. Our second miracle came when the once obstructive property company decided to waive the service charge and rental. This expensive unit was suddenly free of charge! Then came our third miracle. An acquaintance of Robin's, and Tear Fund representative, Peter Kerley, agreed to supply about £3,000 worth of Tearcraft stock. We were off!

The shop itself was large and extremely long, but initially we only used a small frontal section. We were staffed by volunteers from our church, most of them new converts. The vision that God had given me was to reason about the Lord with all who came in there. At first, it was very tough. It was almost as if there were an invisible presence trying to stir up trouble and push us out of the place. But we persevered and witnessed to many people;

and again I learned that just because God gives us the leading to do something, it is not always going to happen without a fight of faith.

'Let's sell second-hand clothes,' said Helen, a staff member. 'It will draw more people into the shop!' I tried not to let it show on my face, but I wasn't going to buy this idea! I had never bought second-hand things, and I hated the idea of selling them. However, the idea grew on me; and, once established, it proved to be a turning point. Sales increased, along with the witness of Christ. Add to this a coffee bar, a work-bench and a prayer room, and you have the unit functioning almost fully.

One morning, some months later, an eviction notice came through my letter box. Another fight of faith had just started. After only six months in operation, they wanted us out. Prayer and lengthy negotiations followed, but they were adamant that they wanted us to leave.

One Christian visitor brought us a word from the Lord: 'You're staying!' they said. I felt that God had said that the unit would exist for two years, but it now seemed impossible.

The fourth miracle, though, was about to surface. The landlords had a change of heart and agreed to let us stay if we paid a modest rent and service charge. What a wonderful victory! We saw more than thirty commitments to Christ made in the shop. A number of people joined the church as a result of the shop and hundreds heard the good news; and, as a non-profit-making charity, we were able to give some money away to international Christian organisations. We were able to support a fifteen-year-old girl who had been abandoned by her parents as a small child. It's staggering what £100 can do in a developing country!

Mandy, whom I mentioned at the start of this story, is a single parent who had moved to Wembley a year earlier. Fraud, drugs and a prison sentence had forced her to seek

a new start. It was wonderful to see her responding to
God's love. Luke, the resident evangelist, had witnessed
to her. Luke just loved people, and Mandy kept coming
along until one day she accepted Jesus as her personal
Saviour. She had continued to grow in her faith and at
one time had worked part-time in the shop, sharing her
story with others there.

We have talked to Hindus, Muslims, Buddhists, non-
believers in any religion, so-called 'religious people',
alcoholics, crooks and just ordinary people going about
their everyday lives. It has been fascinating watching the
Lord move in every situation. We have been threatened
and cursed, but remain unharmed. We have been stretched
to the limit, but never broken.

One of the key people at the shop, Helen, was in effect
made to leave by the government when they refused to
grant her any benefit because she was doing voluntary
work. With her benefit threatened, she had to leave, as
this was her only income. Helen applied for a social care
course at the local job centre and was duly accepted.
The course consisted of nursery work and helping the
physically disabled and mentally handicapped in chosen
work placements. After about two months, the course
extended its criteria to include the homeless and working
with people who had addictions. Helen's placement was
the Open Door, where she became the manageress, paid
for by the government who initially sought to remove
her! This was a fifth miracle and a great testimony to
the mighty works of the Lord in our lives.

I believe in a creative God who gives exciting, creative
ideas. Life is full, never boring, with our wonderful and
adventurous God.

However, don't be too intense or so serious that people
will be put off. Make sure you have some fun. Very few
of those you meet will listen to a preacher. But as you

sweat, laugh or train together, they will listen to you. Go for it!

FOR FURTHER THOUGHT

• Make a list of what you have 'at hand' that you can use for God – home, talents, etc. Then make another list of activities and places you visit regularly: shops, petrol station, workplace, the crèche, pubs, being a cosmetics representative, prayer walks.

• Spend time in prayer asking the Holy Spirit to show you how he wants you to use these opportunities for witnessing.

• Ask him for a creative idea for your church. Do it and persist until you have a breakthrough.

FOR GROUP DISCUSSION

Aim of the Chapter
By the end of the meeting, participants will:

1 Have a better understanding of the creativity that is possible in evangelism.

2 Have generated and evaluated their own creative ideas and those of others, and selected some for use in their own situation.

3 Have thought about starting evangelistic projects (like opening a Christian shop) as a form of outreach.

Key Scriptures
Read and meditate on the following Scriptures. Underline or make a note of verses that particularly speak to you.

1 *Jeremiah 33:3*: Call to me and I will answer you and tell you great and unsearchable things you do not know.

2 *John 10:27*: My sheep listen to my voice; I know them, and they follow me.

Group Participation
Respond individually and as a group (as appropriate) to the following questions/prompting:

1 How has the chapter you have read inspired you to be a creative witness to the gospel?

2 What ideas from the book do you think you could/will use in your own witness?

3 What has struck you most about the section on the Open Door charity shop? Do you think this would work in your locality? How would your church like to be the instigator of such a form of outreach? How would the attitude of local non-Christians change towards the church if it did start such a project?

Prayer
Pray as a group and individually (as appropriate) the following prayers:

1 Dear Lord. Thank you that you are so creative and that your creative nature lives in me. Thank you that I have the mind of Christ and can use it to apply your creativity in my circumstances. Thank you that you have given me all that I have at hand and want me to use it to advance your kingdom. Holy Spirit, help me this week to think of, grasp hold of, and put into practice all the ideas you give me. Thank you again. Amen.

2 That every church would have at least one creative project reaching out to those in its community.

Action
1 Make a list of what you have that you can use for God.

Make another list of those places you regularly go to that you could use to build relations with non-Christians. Also, a list some of the creative ways you have witnessed in the past.

2 With the group or your partner, discuss what has struck you most about what you have read and heard this session. Talk about the ideas/things/places you are now going to use for witnessing and under what circumstances.

3 As a group, 'brainstorm' new creative ways to witness, and to use what you have at hand to create opportunities to witness in word and/or deed. Draw the best ideas from the lists you have just generated to contribute to the group brainstorming session, but don't let this distract you from throwing spontaneous new ideas into the pot as well! Who knows, perhaps the Holy Spirit has chosen you specifically to contribute his idea for the group?

4 As a group, 'brainstorm' creative ideas of an 'Open Door' type. (The list below may spark some new ideas.)

5 Split into four (say) small groups. Each group has the task of preparing a 'presentation' for their church leaders to propose one of the following ideas: (a) a Christian bookshop; (b) a Christian craft shop; (c) a Christian second-hand goods shop; (d) a Christian meeting/eating place; (e) a Christian advice centre; (f) a Christian helpline; (g) a Christian crèche; (h) a Christian baby-sitting service; (i) a Christian help-the-aged-in-practical-ways service; (j) an abortion advice centre; (k) an AIDS helpline on how to prevent AIDS; (l) a 'Your Family Counts' advice service to guide people seeking to reduce family conflicts, offer training in communication skills, give advice on how to work towards reconciliation following separation; or (m) any other idea that the group has come up with earlier.

Each presentation should cover the following topics:

(i) What the idea is.

(ii) Why it will be a blessing to the local community.

(iii) Why spending church funds on this project is justified (compared to other ways of spending), and how the necessary funds will be raised.

(iv) The role for voluntary workers from the church.

(v) How other churches in the area will be blessed (including how unity in the body of Christ will be increased in the area).

(vi) Its impact on other Christian activities in the locality (including any 'competing' Christian initiatives in your area).

Suggestions for Group Leaders

• Before the meeting, you will need to think of some creative evangelistic ideas to encourage the group if it is a little slow to cotton on to what you are trying to accomplish.

• You need to create a 'brainstorming' atmosphere in the group to help people come up with creative ideas. You may need to rearrange things a bit to encourage this. Make the seating as informal as possible. Discourage the participants from being evaluative (that is, judging, thinking of objections, etc.) about ideas. Instead, they need to be constructive (that is, letting one idea, however imperfect, act as a trigger to generate other ideas from other group members). Have some paper/flip chart or a black/white board available to jot down ideas as they are thrown out by the group. Don't be afraid of silence as the group thinks about ideas: a long 'pregnant' silence works wonders in encouraging a group to start talking!

(*Note*: We call this kind of meeting a 'green light meeting' – in other words, anything goes! Any subject can be discussed. However, you need to discourage any correction of others, any emphasis on the 'how to do' of the idea, and 'pouring cold water over visionaries' is defininely out! Let people be as free as possible to express their ideas, however 'wacky' they may seem. You'll be surprised at how many ideas come straight from the heart of God, even though some may have picked up a bit of human 'wackiness' on the way! Trust that God is big enough to let the fleshly and inappropriate ideas die while *his* ideas will float to the top of the priority list and find favour with everyone.

• Why not have a quick group evaluation session after the brainstorming? To do this, ask each member of the group to write down the three ideas they think are most valuable and then get each person to call them out. Score a tick on the white board against each idea every time it is mentioned, then summarise by ranking the ideas in order of popularity.

• A temptation may be to get stuck into the presentation, at the expense of hearing God's voice. Remember to give people the time, and help to create a prayerful atmosphere, to allow the group to get close to God. They *must* hear his creative ideas for them personally and receive his assurance and encouragement to put them into practice, before they launch into the project work.

• If they feel uncertain about hearing God's voice, encourage them to re-read the section on 'How to hear God' on p. 83.

It is part of your task and privilege as a leader to help and encourage the group to open up to hearing and recognising God's voice. Encourage people to speak out 'their' thoughts and guide them towards discerning whether this is a 'Godly' thought or not. Encourage them to 'take risks' and speak from their 'intuition', not just from their minds. Get them used to prefacing

such intuitive statements with 'I feel God may be saying
. . .' or 'Does this make sense to you . . . ?' (Discourage
the 'Thus says the Lord . . .' brand of prophetic utterance.
This is more often used in a manipulative way – that is,
'Who can argue with this if God is speaking through
me?'—than in a truly prophetic way.)

• Try to avoid giving the group the impression that you
are an expert in hearing God clearly, because some will
mistakenly interpret this to mean that, until they are as
mature as you are in the faith, they can't hear God's
voice clearly for themselves. This just isn't true, as you
know well.

• During the week following this meeting, pray that
God's ideas will prevail and that silly ideas will die.
If you think it is appropriate, postpone the group session
for a week and replace it with a 'red light meeting'. This
is when the ideas generated in the meeting go through
an evaluation, prioritising and polishing process. The
practical and experienced people – who may not have
been very good at generating creative idea – can now
comment on how to put the ideas into practice and point
out the weaknesses of the truly unhelpful suggestions.

But lead the meeting with sensitivity. Ideas are sometimes treated very personally, and you need to minimise
the hurt felt when someone's cherished ideas are not
praised by everyone else.

You will find that a meeting of this nature allows people
to run with their own ideas and vision more readily than
those handed down to them from their leaders. Very often,
what God has put in leaders' hearts will also be expressed
by the group in a 'green light meeting', and, then, of
course, you won't have to work hard at motivating people
to pursue the idea!

7

THE SHARING CHURCH

Most churches want to grow, but many do not recognise that their mission field is already within the church. In this chapter and Chapter 8, I want to look at means of evangelism that allow even those who are not naturally outgoing to pull together as they focus on comforting and converting non-believers.

The first (and perhaps only!) key is love, expressed in the unity of the believers, which flows out and draws in others. Colin Urquhart has recounted how people learned to share their lives with each other in a parish church in Luton (*When the Spirit Comes*, Hodder & Stoughton, 1974). It was a period of great revival, as people loved each other and saw their needs met. In that church, everyone who was prayed for over an eighteen-month period received healing. Everything is possible with God!

If you have been rehearsing your testimony recently, you should have recalled your conversion. Like me, I am sure you can remember what it was about Christians that attracted you – and also, perhaps, those aspects of church life that were less appealing!

I am deeply aware that without the care I received in a local church, I would not know Christ today. It began when three women and God ganged up on me – I didn't stand a chance! At work I had met Joyce, my future wife, and one of our senior nursing staff members, both of whom were committed Christians. Then Joyce's mother visited from West Malaysia and took on my case! Everywhere I turned, females were talking with me, praying for me, and encouraging me to receive Christ. What chance did I, a mere mortal, have against such overwhelming odds?

A loving church

On my first visit to a live, Bible-believing church, I was ready to respond to the message. I opened my heart and received Christ as my personal Saviour.

I had been to other churches from time to time, but had always found them boring. The sombre suits, dark pews and a lack of friendliness had worked to form a negative mind-set within me about churches and church people. This church, though, was different. It throbbed with life; an encompassing, pulsating sense of love was in the atmosphere.

The place was full of young people singing, clapping and having a joyful time. It blew my mind! The tangible presence of God started to melt away all my negative thinking about Christianity. 'I want what they have,' I thought. This was very far from being dull – a million light years away from being boring!

The pastor, Robin Rees, preached with conviction, Welsh humour and fire. He was preaching from the heart, unlike those who preached from the head the platitudes of reason that neither stirred my soul nor made much sense. Robin proclaimed the good news – Christ has died, Christ has risen, Christ will come again. God's Son has paid the full price for our free pardon. That day I sought forgiveness with heaving sobs of repentance. At last, I had come home.

I surrendered that day. For many years I had felt unclean, polluted and guilty, but now I was clean. Robin Rees helped me burn three big boxes of occult books: the occult powers of spiritualism, Rosicrucianism, palmistry and astrology (to name but a few) were burnt out of my life. I had been set free through a sharing church.

As a local church, we involved ourselves with street evangelism, visiting hospitals, old people's homes and going from door to door. What a privilege to preach and proclaim the good news! It was difficult to understand why all the churches were not doing this form of witnessing.

This was my 'training college'. Sometimes people want a big ministry right away, but there is usually a process to follow through before we are given such a ministry. Small assignments, well handled, usually lead to bigger projects and more responsibility.

Right attitudes towards leaders

If the body is to work together, it must be united. Seven months after my own conversion, a fresh challenge emerged. I began to realise that church people were not perfect; I saw many things that were obviously wrong. It was like the rug being pulled from under my feet. The false foundation I had relied upon was swiftly and skilfully removed. In fact, I was so discouraged that I almost left the church. Why didn't I see or consider my own faults instead?

A preacher once reasoned that all church people look on the surface like angels with wings, but a closer inspection shows that they are not wings – only their shoulder blades sticking out! There were two factions in our church: those for the pastor and those against. I was a Christian of seven months and had supported and involved myself with the first of these groups – the loyal, faithful group supporting the man of God, the pastor.

With my anti-authority and rebellious background, however, I gradually began to move towards the second, critical and rebellious group. Soon, the pastor's faults and failings were regularly discussed and meditated upon, leading to open opposition of his ministry. This continued for a short while until God stepped in and dealt with me.

In one of our prayer meetings, I opened my eyes. (This was something I never did in those days!) 'I looked directly at the pastor, and God supernaturally showed me his heart. It was pure – 100 per cent committed to God. He was not perfect, but he was a man after God's own heart. 'Serve him,' the Lord said to me. From that day on, I tried my best to do so. No longer rebellious, I encouraged the new converts to join the pastor's Bible studies. God knew that this sin of rebellion had to be broken early on so that my own ministry would have the right foundation.

If I had not responded to God and allowed him to deal with my anti-authority, rebellious past, there would have been no foundation for the glorious future ministry he had for me.

Temptation for new believers

Ten months after I became a Christian, the devil set me up for a big fall. A new girl had come to work on our ward and I immediately started to witness to her. Tracy showed a genuine interest, so I invited her to church. After church, she ran me home in her car. We stopped for a while. I was still saying some things about God to her when she blurted out, 'What I really want is to go to bed with you. I think you are terrific.'

To say I was startled would be an understatement. I got out of that car and ran away from Tracy as fast as I could. You could say, 'What a wimp!', but she was a very attractive girl and my life was not totally sorted out. I was a young, immature Christian. If I had not run – got away from her – I might have fallen into sin.

I have noticed the same pattern, over many years. Those who really respond to Jesus and are zealous for him seem to face challenges in the area of sexual temptation. In 1 Corinthians 10:13, the Bible says that no temptation has overtaken man, except that which is common to man. It adds that God is *faithful*, that he will not let you be tempted above that which you can bear, but will provide a way of escape along with the temptation. Some start out strong and, sadly, fall on the way. The challenge is before us. All are tempted at some point, but God is faithful. His grace is available to overcome.

Will you be one who runs away from such temptations, keeping pure in a polluted generation? It is foundational for all ministry. Here are some helpful hints on how to overcome the temptations of lust:

1 Distance yourself from the place of temptation. Being alone with a person of the opposite sex in a bedroom or car – even to pray – is not a good place to be.

2 Meditate on – chew over, think about – and learn Scripture. 'I have hidden your word in my heart that I might not sin against you' (Ps. 119:11).

3 Decide to be obedient to God in your choice of a life partner. Do not look at what is external only; what counts is not how beautiful or handsome the person is. The important questions to ask yourself are: Do they know God? Do they know how to pray? Do they know how to hear God's voice? Have they got 'the fire'? If not, look for another partner.

141

4 Think from an eternal perspective. You may only be spending ten to twenty years as an ambassador for Christ on earth, whereas stories depicting victories of the devil – such as Samson and Delilah, and David and Bathsheba – are still being flaunted in the cinemas some three thousand years later. In contrast, thousands of years later, too, Joshua, Caleb and Jesus are still talked about as those who had the spirit of faith. Decide to be pure before God. Be someone who is remembered for their godly life.

5 Draw daily on God's grace, his divine help in overcoming temptation. He is faithful and will provide you with a way of escape! (1 Cor. 10:13.)

Being a friend to the lonely

The women who befriended me and witnessed to me before I became a Christian taught me how important it is for individual church members to reach out to people who do not know Jesus. On the outside, I was Mr Cool, but on the inside I was lonely.

Both the world and the Church are full of lonely people; loneliness is the No. 1 problem in today's Western society. Sadly, many Christians are ready to witness, but not to alter their lifestyle to become a friend to someone who wants to take up their time, whereas plenty of cults and other religions have hospitality programmes to meet these needs for friendship.

'Why did you become a Muslim?' one newspaper article asked a new convert to Islam. The answer was, 'Well, they have some ideas that I don't agree with, but it is the friendship. I used to go to church, but after the service everybody just went home, so I stopped going.'

Sadly, the case of one woman who explained to me that she had been going to church for five months but nobody

142

had really talked to her, was not unique. Even in church, most of us gravitate towards those who appear kind and friendly, but you should be prepared for those who come in off the street, those who are rejected and broken-hearted and may not be the easiest of people to talk to.

If somebody is lonely, they need to know the comfort that only God can bring. But unless someone speaks to them, they will not hear about him. *We* know that Jesus is willing to become their friend, but *they* do not know that. Until they discover that, you may be the only friend they ever meet. In nursing, I found that some patients have no family and never receive a visitor.

A smile or a cheerful, encouraging word and a listening ear can become part of our lifestyle. Don't be patronising; the lonely or rejected are adept at sensing insincerity. Sometimes lonely or rejected people are sullen and with-drawn; others are extremely talkative.

Very often, if the lonely are given time, they will allow you to share your faith with them. It's amazing to see how many brighten up if the love of Jesus is communicated to them. They need to know that Jesus invites them to come to him if they are weary and burdened, because he will give them rest (Matt. 11:28). There are specific Scriptures to share with these people: 'Yet to all who received him, to those who believed in his name, he gave the right to become children of God . . .' (John 1:12). '[Jesus said] And surely I am with you always, to the very end of the age' (Matt. 28:20b).

However, some lonely people are not easy to relate to and you may have to be prepared for rejection. One man I led to the Lord at church told me that during his three months of visits, only three of us had talked to him. Yet he was not an easy person to approach. In these circumstances, you pray before you go to speak to someone. Once you have established a rapport, introduce them to others.

When counselling someone after a church service, sharpen your listening skills! If a person has been brought to the service, participated in praise and worship, heard an hour's sermon and prayers, and decided to respond to an altar call, they will not respond well to more preaching when you begin to counsel them afterwards. In fact, you may never see them again. But you *can* gently pose a question: 'What was it in the service that appealed to you?'

Do listen carefully to people's replies, because they may well indicate a need in their life. Two obvious examples are healing and the provision of money. If the person replies to your initial question, 'Yes, the way that person got that money was good', you know immediately that they probably have that need themselves.

At this point, you could preach an hour's sermon to them, but I prefer to ask them questions to elicit details about their need. This is especially important during a church service.

Of course, they may tell you all the things they *didn't* like, but keep your sense of humour: 'What were all those people doing on the floor?' 'Oh, that was the power of God at work.' 'Don't be drawn into an explanation of being 'slain in the Spirit', but return to the person's own needs and situation: 'Did anything speak to you in the service?'

Then you must listen, which doesn't come naturally to extroverts! At this point, I've seen some evangelists make the mistake of metaphorically spraying people with gospel bullets; they have an audience and off they go, mowing down their listener with words. When they've finished and their target is full of bullet holes, they move on to the next one, filling them full of lead! They have made the primary mistake of not meeting people at their point of need.

Once the person has acknowledged what affected them, ask, 'Did you know that God can do the same for you?' Give them your testimony at this point, but keep it brief, because they have already heard the sermon.

Taking the time to befriend someone may mean a change of lifestyle, but it is essential if the Church is to back up its words and be seen to live out what it says it believes. As believers we can emphasise the power of God's word to change lives, but the rest of the world is always looking for the evidence.

Jesus *commanded* us to love one another, saying that this love will prove we are his disciples; it is certainly the secret to winning and keeping the lonely.

Is your church visitor friendly?

It is not only the lonely who need special attention. Some churches can make the most sociable people feel unwanted. If you have ever been to a church where no one talked to you, this may sound familiar.

The impression your church makes on visitors starts in the car park. Are there spaces reserved for visitors? If you have a parking attendant, are they friendly or do they growl and fuss about 'their' car park?

An American, Ken Houts, has made a study of church visiting patterns in the United States. He visited our church at Kingdom Faith to share the results with us and, in doing so, a strategic ministry emerged: the 'Care Ministry'.

Ken has discovered that 15 per cent of visitors join a church and 15 per cent reject it, usually within the first fourteen minutes, leaving 70 per cent undecided. Another statistic: unless someone finds seven friends in the first five months of being at a church, they leave. Here lies your mission field.

Care Ministry

Ken's visit to our church gave birth to the most consistently fruitful ministry I have seen in a local church. With
around a hundred visitors a month, we could not afford to
ignore his advice. The Care Ministry has grown to a major
ministry in our church; many have responded and become
believers through it, while existing believers have been
comforted through the love and prayer of Care Ministry
team members showing a genuine interest in them and
their families. Others have been healed and delivered
through the team's ministry.

In 1995 the Care Ministry was a major contributor
to our growth, bringing thirty new converts to Christ a
month; at present, commitments are about ten a month.
Whether or not people join the church, we believe we have
succeeded if they have been shown the love of Jesus.

Initially we asked for volunteers for the new Care
Ministry and used Ken Houts's cassettes and books to
train them (see the Resources List at the back of the
book). Some 8 to 10 per cent of our people volunteered;
the majority are ordinary believers rather than leaders or
the usual nucleus.

Care Ministry operation

Our groups meet before the service to pray, asking God
to bless the visitors. Afterwards, a few will greet visitors
as they arrive. The rest have designated seats in the
auditorium. Each team member looks after a given area
and will pray over it, taking authority over ungodly spirits
and praying that the Holy Spirit will fill that area.

During the service, the leader on the platform will
publicly welcome the visitors and pray for them. The

team member passes duplicate cards and pens to the visitors, which the leader encourages them to fill in there and then and hand back to the team member, who is waiting at the end of the row. Very few people refuse to fill in the cards, which ask simply for the visitor's name, address and telephone number (if they wish to give it), and if there is anything they would like us to pray for them (in confidence).

Just before the service concludes, team members stand at the end of the row to greet the visitor. The team member smiles and gives a warm handshake, saying words on the lines of, 'My name is . . . Are you visiting us for the first time today?' They then escort them to the coffee and tea table (which is free to visitors), and they are then welcome to sit at the table and talk with the visitor if they wish to do so.

Many of the visitors who arrive in churches these days are battered by both life and the devil's schemes. We believe God has brought them to us to meet the God of miracles. Ken has the motto, 'My availability is God's opportunity to do a miracle through me'. The team will ask, 'Is there anything I can pray about for you?' This helps people to open their hearts, often with amazing results.

Naturally we have had to meet challenges week by week in this work. This is what we have done to solve three of them:

Challenge 1 Not enough visitors
Solution: Go and show love to an existing church member.

Challenge 2 Too many visitors
Solution: This is difficult to solve on the day, unless the rest of the church helps. The long-term solution is to recruit more team members.

Challenge 3 Follow-up

• We aim to visit people within forty-eight hours of their coming to church for the first time, but our twenty-five-mile radius target area proved too large for the team to visit people mid-week.

Solution: God's wisdom was to prompt us to create evangelistic representatives from the various areas within the radius.

We have seen excellent responses to the representatives' visits; it tells the person that they are appreciated. If the person has just given their life to Christ, we aim to visit within twenty-four hours, because they will be surrounded by unbelievers and must be encouraged.

'Commitment to Christ'

I prefer the expression 'commitment to Christ' to 'born again', because sometimes people express a commitment without having encountered God. Therefore I never assume someone is 'born again'. As we follow up people, we soon discover whether or not they have 'the fruits of repentance' – that is, the beginning of a changed life through repentance of sin. If someone has opened their heart to God and let him change them, it will become evident to all over the weeks or months. Until then, I keep seeking to introduce them lovingly to the Saviour.

Once one of our area representatives received a follow-up card which stated that a man and woman had made a commitment to Christ. On visiting them, she realised that in fact neither had, although one of them had already had an ulcer instantly healed. That miracle allowed our worker to speak freely of Christ, and that night one of them gave their life to God. The following week, I accompanied the representative and the other partner responded in a dramatic way. The fruit of their encounters with God emerged in repentance and a change of lifestyle; they got married and are now fully committed to God and each other.

The Care Ministry continues to grow and develop to the extent that I have been able to delegate its leadership to others while I seek to develop other ministries within the church. Your church may receive more or fewer visitors than ours, but this ministry will still work in your setting.

I pray that all churches will reach out and love the stranger in their midst, that they will move out from their cliques and go to church to bless, to give, to love.

SUMMARY

These are tests that people either overcome or fail:

• *Matthew 28:19*: Jesus commands us to *go*. Obey this command and refuse to compromise your witness to Christ.

• *1 Peter 5:5*: The younger submit to the elders. Pass the tests of humility when the Lord uses us, as Joseph did. We must humble ourselves to imperfect leadership. (I am not referring to cults or groups that practise 'heavy shepherding' – that is, controlling members' lives. It is best to leave them immediately and find a good church.)

• *1 Corinthians 3:1–8*: Make a decision that, 'I am of Christ and I will follow him', no matter what the other church members do or say, regardless of how shallow or critical others may be. 'I have decided to follow Jesus, no turning back, no turning back', as the song goes! This attitude produces marvellous character traits. Jesus himself was betrayed, deserted, criticised and misunderstood. He learned obedience through the things he suffered. It is easy to be obedient when all is well, but to trust and obey in the middle of the storm or hard trial enables us to know God. His grace, power and love deliver us and we know it is not us but him. We can only boast in him and marvel at his grace, as again and again he goes on saving us! Follow him, regardless of the church, regardless of others. He will never con you and never let you down. He tells us no lies, nor does he break promises. What love!

• Jesus commands us to love one another and lay down our lives for each other (John 15:12–13). If we are serious about church unity and church growth, this is the only way that we will achieve it.

FOR GROUP DISCUSSION

Aim of the Chapter
By the end of the meeting, participants will have:

1 A better understanding of the role of the local church, working together to make disciples of all people.

2 The opportunity to face up to some of the issues that can hinder new (and not-so-new!) Christians becoming effective members of the local church.

Key Scriptures
Read and meditate on the following Scriptures. Underline or make a note of verses that particularly speak to you.

1 *Matthew 28:19*: Therefore go and make disciples of all nations, baptising them in the name of the Father and of the Son and of the Holy Spirit.

2 *1 Peter 5:5–6:* Young men, in the same way be submissive to those who are older. All of you, clothe yourselves with humility towards one another, because 'God opposes the proud but gives grace to the humble.'

150

Humble yourselves, therefore, under God's mighty hand, that he may lift you up in due time.

3 *1 Corinthians 3:1–8*: Brothers, I could not address you as spiritual but as worldly – mere infants in Christ. I gave you milk, not solid food, for you were not yet ready for it. Indeed, you are still not ready. You are still worldly. For since there is jealousy and quarrelling among you, are you not worldly? Are you not acting like mere men? For when one says, 'I follow Paul,' and another, 'I follow Apollos,' are you not mere men? What, after all, is Apollos? And what is Paul? Only servants, through whom you came to believe – as the Lord has assigned to each his task. I planted the seed, Apollos watered it, but God made it grow. So neither he who plants nor he who waters is anything, but only God, who makes things grow. The man who plants and the man who waters have one purpose, and each will be rewarded according to his own labour.

4 *John 15:12–13*: My command is this: Love each other as I have loved you. Greater love has no-one than this, that he lay down his life for his friends.

Group participation
Respond individually and as a group (as appropriate) to the following questions/prompting:

1 What, in your own experience, builds up your church most? What tears it down? Are you primarily a church builder or destroyer? Do you work in harmony with others to expand the kingdom of God? Are you trying to produce the growth in your own strength? Are you proud of your effective service for the Lord? Or does God really get all the credit?

2 Are you one of those who (mainly) supports and encourages your pastor and other members of the church, or are you among those who generally think and speak negatively about him/them? What are the consequences of this attitude – on your pastor, on yourself and on others in your church? Does your attitude help or hinder your ability to be an effective witness to the gospel? What does God want you to do?

3 Does your church or fellowship's unity express itself to strangers? What could you do to make people feel more welcome in your meetings?

Prayer
Pray as a group and individually (as appropriate) the following prayers:

1 For help in obediently and trustingly *going out* and witnessing; and for help in overcoming the fears and other things that prevent you from witnessing. (If you know the reasons, tell the group and ask them to pray for you in dealing with these problems. If you don't understand why, invite the group to ask God for revelation as to how you can overcome this barrier you are up against.)

2 If you need prayer for proud, unsubmissive, divisive and critical attitudes towards others in your church (especially the pastor), pray (out loud is best) – confessing, repenting and asking forgiveness as the Spirit leads you. Ask God to remove all the negative attitudes in your heart and replace them with his positive attitude, and his thoughts and words.

3 Forgive in prayer those whom you know or suspect have been critical, judgmental and proud in their relations with you. Ask the Holy Spirit to show you if you need to tell them you have forgiven them. (If he does, make sure you don't forgive in a proud, critical or judgmental way!)

4 For unity in the church/churches in your locality and a heart to witness to the world. Pray in faith that every

Christian in your area will become a fruitful 'friendship evangelist'. (Before you pray this prayer, you need to be willing to show your faith – that is, that God has heard and answered your prayer – by *going out* and loving and witnessing to at least one non-Christian this coming week.)

5 For a willing heart to welcome visitors into your church and your life, even at the expense of altering current social groupings.

Action
With their neighbour, or openly if the group is small, each group member should:

1 Talk through the issues identified, honestly, humbly and repentantly (if necessary).

2 Spend three minutes telling your partner/the group the best (that is, the most positive) things you have noticed about your pastor and your own church.

3 Discuss the possibility of forming a 'Care Ministry' team for welcoming, praying with and visiting new people.

Suggestions for group leaders
• This is going to be a challenging session, so be prepared to teach on the need for unity, submission, forgiveness and positiveness towards all other Christians. This is such an important issue that we all need to receive this truth and act on it.

• If it is a problem that *you personally* have, make sure you have got right with others/your pastor etc. before you lead the meeting.

• Be prepared to be encouraging to those who are struggling with Jesus's command to go and be a witness, and to make sure that others are encouraging too. Resist firmly all critical and judgmental attitudes in those who have overcome their fear to witness towards those who are still struggling. Remember when the group/individuals are asked to seek God for revelation about why a fellow Christian is having difficulty, that the heart and word of God is *always* to edify and build up his people. Words that bring condemnation, rather than conviction, *are not from God but from Satan.*

• Be prepared to be uncompromising and challenging. We all love to wriggle around the truth if it hurts. You won't be doing anyone any favours if you let them do so. But remember that God only reveals our faults, and the deceptions that conceal them from us, when we are ready to face up to them. You need the sensitivity and help of the Holy Spirit in discerning when to challenge and when to refrain. You need to prepare yourself well in prayer before this session.

8

PUTTING THE HEART INTO IT

Generally, in any church, only a small number of people love evangelism. They usually do it without much support from the leadership or body of the church and the devil has another success in easing evangelism to one side.

There are also many churches that encourage evangelism, and some have an evangelistic group. It often consists of a small, committed nucleus of people working on the sidelines of the church; some of these are already stretched to breaking point. There is also the threat of division and dissension if such a group, working in isolation, is tempted to judge the rest of the church for not evangelising.

God wants evangelism to flow naturally through the heart of a church, as much an expression of his life as loving relationships are within the body of Christ. For this to happen, the leadership – especially the overall leader – must have a vision for it and be seen to be supportive, even if someone else is appointed to lead the work.

The answer in my experience has been evangelism through the network of home groups. Churches gather to celebrate together in the main weekly meetings, yet people rarely get to know one another or form intimate friendships. Smaller meetings, which usually take place in people's homes, are needed to effect this bonding. God has raised these home groups – also known as life or cell groups – all over the world. David Yonggi Cho says this is the secret of his church's phenomenal growth in Korea (there are several hundred thousand members), but some churches with home groups have become inward-looking.

I received the vision for evangelism through home groups in a dramatic way. After returning in 1979 from south-east Asia where revival was underway, our arrival in London was very depressing. The nation and the Church were in the doldrums. At St Mark's, Kennington, we were already aware of the need to evangelise in obedience to Jesus's command. One day, God told me to take the church out into the parish to do door-to-door evangelism. He revealed the strategy: the reorganisation of our home groups.

By altering our calendar, we were able to hold twelve prayer meetings, twelve evangelistic meetings, and four social/evangelistic events a year without adding one extra meeting to the church calendar. Instead of having four teaching/pastoral meetings a month, we changed the format. A map of the parish was divided into sections and we allocated one section to each group.

The first week we would pray, pray and pray for our patch. Some of the groups went out 'prayer walking' in their area. On the fourth week, the church people went out into their area to speak of Christ door to door.

The remaining two weeks were for pastoral care and teaching. We also restructured the morning service, turning it into an open invitation meeting. This Anglican church was bold enough to put aside the liturgy and allow the Holy Spirit to have freedom to move.

In each quarter there is a five-week month. We were able to turn this 'extra' evening into a social/evangelistic event such as a barn dance, a 'Bring and Share', an Afro-Caribbean evening, or an open-air barbecue. Every six weeks we had a 'Bring and Share' on a Sunday afternoon and regularly saw the invited people from the parish give their lives to the Lord. (The 'Bring and Share' is explained in Chapter 6.)

Many non-Christians will come to such events. The purpose here was not to 'jump' on the visitors and metaphorically 'club them to death with the gospel', but to allow them to see that Christians are normal and can have fun. Visitors who had believed that all Christians were weird and boring often expressed their surprise to me at these events! The church grew from 100 to 500 members.

St Mark's was well known in the area, having its own church school, and a magazine, *Crossroads*, that church members had delivered locally for several years. Now it was easy to deliver a copy of the magazine personally or to say 'I'm from St Mark's' or 'I'm from the Sunday school' (which some parents let their children attend). Although some church members were frightened of visiting homes in rough areas and numbers dwindled on visiting nights, those who dared to obey the command to go into all of Kennington were tremendously encouraged.

The following passage by Jenny Cooke gives some more detail:

At the height of the visiting campaign, Jeffrey Fewkes, the curate, noted that up to 250 church members would be out visiting per month. The leaders all felt this was fantastic. The church persevered with its visiting for over eighteen months until by 1981 every home in the parish, over three thousand of them, was being visited monthly . . .

During prayer they believed earnestly that God's wind would blow over Kennington. Gradually they came to a consensus that they should believe for

157

ten new converts a month. As the months went by the startling thing was that, slowly but surely, that target was being reached. And at least 50 per cent of the newcomers lived in the parish. Every six weeks there was an evangelistic service and people were able to bring along those who had shown an interest during the visiting evenings (*Upon this Rock* by Jenny Cooke, Hodder & Stoughton, 1989).

Favour with the community

Acts 2 states that the believers 'received favour with the community' – so did we! It started with a bomb scare one night in our area. The police evacuated many houses and blocks of flats. The people were outside in the cold at 2 o' clock in the morning. The local councillors could not be called because they lived outside the area. Our vicar, Nicholas Rivett-Carnac, came and opened the church and hundreds of cold and somewhat bemused people spent part of the night huddled together over a cup of tea. You can imagine 'the favour' this gave the church! The word spread like wildfire: 'The vicar opened the church and gave us a cup of tea at 2 a.m.!' So in future, when we knocked on doors, our opening line was, 'We are from St Mark's Church.'

Many thoughts had persisted in my mind about doors being forcibly closed, total failure and rejection. The thoughts that came from the Holy Spirit were very different. He indicated that more doors would be open to us than we could manage. Before we went out on the streets, the negative thoughts were the strongest. After going out, the Holy Spirit's thoughts became stronger. Deception could have immobilised us, but when we acted on the truth it set us free.

Pray over the territory

It is important to combine consistent prayer with proclaiming the gospel. God will give you favour and supernatural signs if you pray and go. Seek his strategy first; currently our church has a project of praying for every single home in our town. It also prays for a twenty-five-mile radius, but – like Joshua, who took one city at a time – we are fighting on one front at a time and focusing on the town where we are situated.

People from the next town are coming over to help us, in the same way that all the tribes of Israel won each other's land together before settling in their own territory. We also join other churches for prayer marching in our town.

So put your foot down on your patch and claim it for God. It will not be easy. There will be those who reject the message, but there will always be some who respond to Jesus, and that makes it all worthwhile.

When I first took the Anglican church out, we were greeted with a great deal of suspicion. No wonder, because Mormons, Moonies, Jehovah's Witnesses, muggers and Communists were all out in the same area! As we perservered, both in visiting and praying, some of the people began to look forward to our visits. Eventually I recognised that this familiarity is God's way of preparing people for the gospel.

People we visited spoke of dreams about God and asked what they might mean. We sometimes prayed for healing and saw instant results right there on the doorstep. More doors were opened to us than we could manage. People began to invite us inside, and many told us of their deep hurts, needs and social problems.

Getting known

Most people in Kennington seemed to know of St Mark's Church; it helped that it was a huge building with traffic swirling round it all day! If you are in a less conspicuous church or fellowship, you may well need to raise its profile in the community. When we were asked by an Assemblies of God pastor to work with them in Wembley a few years later, I learnt a lesson about the importance of getting a church known.

When the great day arrived for my induction as associate pastor of the New Life Christian Centre, excitement gripped me as we made our way to our new church. My parents and many friends were coming to my induction; it was a great honour.

It was a tremendous service and many dear friends were there, but I looked in vain for my parents and family. I found out later that they had been unable to find the church. After asking some local people, they had been directed to the Jehovah's Witnesses' hall and then to the local Anglican church.

In my disappointment, God seemed to nudge me and say, 'Most of the local people don't know where the church is!' It was through my parents' fruitless ninety-minute search for the church that God revealed his first strategy for evangelism in my new post.

On our first outreach we delivered leaflets to 2,300 houses with an invitation to our healing service, stating what kind of church we were and where we were. A map and service times were included, along with a short testimony of God's healing miracles. Ten new people responded to the altar call to give their lives to Christ after the leaflet drop, and the disappointment of not seeing my parents at the induction gave way to excitement. By presenting the church in this way, it gained higher visibility in the community and we continued to receive people from the area of the housing estate.

Somewhat to my surprise, I found the same home group evangelism strategy on my heart at the new church. God seemed to be speaking to me yet again: 'Son, the people don't even know the church is here. I want you to take the people on the doors and tell them the power of God is here and they can be healed on the door or in church.'

The Assemblies of God senior pastor agreed to let me change the format of the three home groups. We adopted the same format as we had used so successfully at St Mark's, dividing up our housing estate of 2,300 houses into three areas, so that each group would spend a whole evening praying for their own area.

So fruitful was the Lord's strategy that we were almost swamped by the very needy people who joined our church. In the first year we had a hundred new Christians, including people recovering from involvement in Satanism or incestuous abuse. It was not unusual to have people threaten suicide down the phone or ring on the doorbell with a problem at 3 o'clock in the morning.

The demands on us of loving all these people drove us to pray for some 'transfer growth' – in other words, mature believers who could come in and help! Soon other Christians joined us and we continued to grow. When we left that church, the three original home groups had been supplanted by many others; we had 300 members and planted two other churches.

In 1994 Joyce and I had the privilege of taking up a new post in Kingdom Faith Church. It is a large church and, again, I joined as associate pastor. Here, we have already seen the same model with the home groups beginning to produce fruit. The groups are reaching out in prayer and witness. The church, which grew to

800 by transfer growth, is now seeing a great many new converts.

We have looked at how your congregation can work together through holding church events; now I want to look at ideas for team witnessing.

Door-to-door evangelism

There are certain groups, like Jehovah's Witnesses, who have grown very quickly through door-to-door witnessing. While we know the Jehovah's Witnesses' message is one of deception, this *method* can produce fruit if we stick to it, although it can be tough.

Go out in twos, like the first disciples. Let one speak while the other prays (there are more hints in Chapter 10 on this subject). Take it in turns to speak, unless one of you has a strong sense that they should speak in a particular place.

Remember to smile – *and* to speak! Those who open the door want to know your reason for calling and many will already be guarded and suspicious, thinking you are a Jehovah's Witness, a Mormon or a con-man. Muggers and thieves are out there, too.

A long, embarrassing silence, and then a stammering and apologetic 'I'm a Christian from such and such a church', will put people off immediately. As they slam the door you may hear, 'I'm a Muslim' or 'I'm a Roman Catholic. I've got my own religion, thank you very much'.

Be polite and reassuring; focus on why you called (an invitation to a healing meeting, for example). After introducing yourself, it is sometimes right to ask, 'Do you believe in God?' or 'Do you go to a place of worship?' The answers can be very revealing and lead to further conversation. We would then say, 'We're doing a survey. Could you spare some time to answer some questions?'

Questionnaires and surveys

These can be a very useful aid for engaging people in conversation on the street, on the doorstep or in public places such as pubs! (See the Appendix at the back of the book.) Have a clipboard, pens and a confident smile ready. As in most things, there is an element of faith involved here; if you have been praying, you can believe that there are people out there who actually *want* to do your survey and hear the gospel.

Don't be afraid that you might accidentally coerce people; if they don't want to do it, they won't! But I always try to have some fun with people, and might tease them a bit, which means that I have to be ready to be teased in return!

Once you have started, there is no need to follow your questionnaire slavishly – it is your servant, not your master. If you don't agree with a person's answer, such as 'Yes, I believe shops should trade on Sundays', for goodness' sake don't start contradicting them and talking about the Lord's day.

Next I take the opportunity to demonstrate the authenticity of the Bible with one of the following anecdotes. Either I ask them, 'Did you know that every week the Bible is the best-selling book in the whole world?' Or I explain that many people have suffered over the centuries for the sake of translating (or even just owning) the Bible, and they are still suffering in China and other repressive countries today. There is also the anecdote about the French philosopher Voltaire, who claimed that after his death, people would read his works rather than the Bible. A hundred years after his death, the Bible Society had turned his home into a Bible printing house – that's God's humour!

Then you can ask people, 'Do you know the best-known verse in the Bible?' Then read them John 3:16. Older people may well recognise it, but younger ones will probably look blank. I explain some of the verse's meaning, beginning with 'God so loved the world, . . .' and explain that Jesus was God's only Son. If appropriate, I give a little of my testimony at this point, explaining how I experienced the truth of this verse in my life.

Assuming you have side-stepped potential arguments, you will reach the last questions, on the lines of 'Do you believe Jesus Christ exists/died on a cross/was resurrected from the dead?' I am often amazed by people's readiness to affirm these truths, even if they do not go to church and dislike religion. A 'yes' to this final question is your opportunity to speak of Jesus.

If they say 'yes' to the question 'Do you believe in God?', it is worth asking in return, 'What's your God like?' Listen carefully before you tell them about *your* God.

Be aware that the enemy would love to side-track you, and he knows exactly what your sensitive points are. Remember that you are reeling in a fish (you're a fisher of men!) and the devil will do all he can to throw up red herrings. Some people you meet will ask *you* question after question, without really wanting any answers; they are just avoiding the real issue of their standing before God.

Or you may find your very personality and identity is attacked, just as Jesus faced: 'If [or *since*] you are the Son of God, tell this stone to become bread . . . [why don't you] throw yourself down from here . . .' (Luke 4:3, 9); '. . . let him save himself if he is the Christ of God, the Chosen One' (Luke 23:35). These were attacks on Jesus's very identity as the Son of God and Saviour of the world, tempting him to misuse his divine power by performing miracles at the moments when he was at his weakest as a human. If he had acceded to these temptations, he would have been acting out of his Father's will – out of the Spirit and in the flesh. The enemy knows that most of the time your soul-winning will stop flowing if you can be tempted to speak or act in the flesh – without waiting for the Holy Spirit's prompting, or out of selfish motives, such as a desire to be 'right'; even if you feel bound to defend your church or the whole Christian Church or God himself from unjust assertions, remember that the point of your encounter is for this person to hear of *God's love* for them.

Jesus demonstrates this beautifully in the encounter with the Samaritan woman; he read people's hearts, but did not always reveal the fact immediately. Hence his request that she should fetch her husband; this request bypassed her other questions, so that of the three thorny political theological questions she asked, he answered only one, the one that focused on her spiritual need.

Argumentative people

Although we all like to win arguments, they are often a smokescreen by the enemy and are intended to steal our time and keep us from those who are genuinely interested in knowing more about Jesus. I tend to keep these exchanges short and move on to the next person.

As I have proved to my cost, you can win a battle and lose the war. Once I went to visit a man who had come to church for a while, then lapsed. He greeted me warmly and we were happily chatting when a Jehovah's Witness whom the man knew arrived. I started talking to the Jehovah's Witness, who challenged me by asserting that tongues and prophecy had passed away.

165

I took up the theological gauntlet, and found myself quoting 1 Corinthians 13:8–10, which claims that these gifts *and knowledge* will pass away *when perfection comes*. The Jehovah's witness agreed that perfection had not yet arrived, but had to return to his elders to find out whether knowledge had passed away! After his departure, rather than my host being open to what I had to share of the gospel, it was clear he felt more empathy towards the departed (and defeated) Jehovah's Witness! I had shared a brilliant revelation, but lost the opportunity of winning that man to Christ.

By God's grace, we have been able to strategise and lead different churches into evangelism. When we started, we programmed each event. As the groups matured and learned on the job, we encouraged them to seek God for creative ideas. Pray about using these ideas in your church and wait on the Lord to hear every detail of his strategy for your church, then implement exactly what the Holy Spirit tells you.

We are used for sowing and watering, but God alone brings about the harvest. Therefore he alone receives all the glory!

SUMMARY

Read Proverbs 29:18, Mark 16:15 and Romans 10:14–15.
• *Vision*: The devil tries to keep evangelism to a select few in the church, but God wants the whole church to be trained and mobilised for effective evangelism.

A healthy group will look outwards. Any group that looks only to its own needs will become stagnant and selfish.

• *Intercessory prayer*: Our area was divided into sections. Each group had their own area to pray for on the first Wednesday of each month. Consistent prayer for each area will drive the enemy out and set up strongholds for the Lord to work through.

• *Door-to-door evangelism*: Every fourth Wednesday we visited and talked to people and leafleted the area before our Healing and Miracle services.

• *Presence evangelism*: We wanted the whole area saturated with God's presence. We wanted the estate to know that the New Life Christian Centre existed and that their needs could be met there by God. God lives in us and we carry his presence wherever we go. As we go, he goes, and where he goes, people get saved!

• *Persuasion*: 'Since, then, we know what it is to fear the Lord, we try to persuade men (2 Cor. 5.11). 'And how can they believe in the one of whom they have not heard? And how can they hear without someone preaching to them? (Rom. 10:14.)

Most of us heard the message many times before we understood and decided to follow Christ. Why should we give up so easily on others because they did not understand or respond the first time we spoke of Jesus with them? To 'persuade' is to 'convince' or 'impel by argument'. This implies a rugged determination to speak of Jesus continually.

• *Proclamation*: We foretell, by announcing publicly to the demonic hordes and to the people. What you sow, you reap. The Word of God is a seed when proclaimed in faith, planted and watered by us. God gives the increase. He produces the harvest. We do our part and God does the rest.

FOUR GROUP DISCUSSION

Aim of the chapter
By the end of the meeting, participants will:

1 Have explored ideas for change in their local church that will (a) increase intercessory prayer (b) encourage the whole church to become witnesses and (c) help the church gain favour with local inhabitants.

2 Have the opportunity for a season of presence and persuasion evangelism through the life of home groups.

Key Scriptures
Read and meditate on the following Scriptures. Underline or make a note of verses that particularly speak to you.

1 *Proverbs 29:18*: Where there is no revelation, the people cast off restraint; but blessed is he who keeps the law.

2 *Romans 10:14–15*: How, then, can they call on the one they have not believed in? And how can they believe in the one of whom they have not heard? And how can they hear without someone preaching to them? And how can they preach unless they are sent? As it is written, 'How beautiful are the feet of those who bring the good news!'

3 *2 Corinthians 5:10–11*: For we must all appear before the judgment seat of Christ, that each one may receive what is due to him for the things done while in the body, whether good or bad. Since, then, we know what it is to fear the Lord, we try to persuade men. What we are is plain to God, and I hope it is also plain to your conscience.

4 *Galatians 6:7*: Do not be deceived: God cannot be mocked. A man reaps what he sows.

Group participation
Respond individually and as a group (as appropriate) to the following questions/prompting:

1 Spend time thinking (jot down your conclusions) about the following questions related to witnessing in your church:

(a) What is/should be your church's vision for outreach and witness? It has been said that if you can't write down your vision, you haven't got one!

(b) What methods of witnessing (or mix of methods) do/might work best in your area (for example, street work, door-to-door visiting, friendship evangelism, etc.)?

(c) What can you do to win favour with the people and change, for the better the (generally negative) image that the Church as a whole has?

(d) How can your home/cell groups (or the whole church body) be more involved in witnessing? Review the model given in the chapter: how might you adapt or implement it?

2 Review again your own commitment to witnessing. Do you know the 'terror of the Lord' regarding those who are under his anger and judgment? Does the fact that they are bound for a Christless eternity stir you into action?

Prayer
Spend much of the session in prayer:

1 Spend time praising the Lord (in words and songs if possible) – for who he is and his authority and power. Praise him for his victory on the cross over all and every spiritual power and authority that would stand in the way of the advance of the kingdom of God. Praise him that the gates of hell (Hades/Sheol) will *not* prevail against the Church. Praise him for the victory he has won over the enemy in your local area. Praise him in faith for those who are going to be won for him in your area in the next few years. Praise him for equipping his people to be overcomers and powerful witnesses for the gospel.

Spend time – as much time as possible – praising and singing in tongues.

2 Spend time proclaiming – confidently and prophetically speaking the truth – the victory that Christ has won over sin, the world and Satan. Tell the enemy what is going to happen in your area and church, and his powerlessness to prevent these prophetic proclamations from being fulfilled.

3 Spend time interceding for non-Christians in your area and for a revival of love for the lost in the local church(es). Seek the will of God – what he wants you to intercede for – before you start praying. If you understand about (and the group is comfortable with) interceding in the Spirit (groaning in intercessory prayer), ask the Holy Spirit, who indwells you, to intercede for your area.

Action
Each group member should:

1 Give his thoughts on how evangelism can become part of the lifestyle in your church (either with another member of the group, or openly to the group if it is small enough).

2 'Prayer walk'. Plan to spend time in the coming week walking a part of your locality to claim it in prayer for the Lord. Make a firm commitment to stick to your plan.

Suggestions for Group Leaders
• Remember to devote much of the meeting to prayer. Pray in the Spirit (in tongues) as much as possible if this is a form of prayer the group is familiar with. If not, take the opportunity to explain (briefly) what it is and to set time aside later to lead the group into this type of prayer. Make use of 'whole group' and 'small group' prayer times for different types of prayer.

• Avoid constant direct and confrontational spiritual warfare – that is, directly 'engaging the enemy'. Follow our suggestion to focus on praise and proclamation as the means of defeating the devil.

• Encourage the group to put into practice in their private prayer times and church prayer groups, the things they have learnt today about praying and spiritual warfare.

9

RIGHT EXPECTATIONS

The Lord says, 'I will build my church' (Matt. 16:18). It is not we, but *he* – not our plans, but *his* plans. God has a blueprint, a strategy, as inferred in Psalm 127, which declares that unless the Lord builds the house, those who labour do so in vain. In everything we seek to do for God, we have to remember that we are not called to work *for him*, but to co-operate and work *with him* as co-heirs with Christ himself (2 Cor. 6:1; Rom. 8:17).

Our vision, goals and expectations are to come out of prayer – out of hearing God's voice and knowing his heart and mind. That closeness will lift you above your feelings and circumstances so that you can have the right expectations in any seemingly unfriendly situation.

When Joyce and I returned from south-east Asia in the early 1980s, we had been in a 'revival situation' for over a year. Almost everything we touched had been wonderfully blessed by God. Hundreds became Christians and were baptised in the Holy Spirit, while many were healed of various diseases.

Mighty miracles were seen through the ministry of others, such as a tumour as big as a football disappearing at the evangelist's command and a dead baby coming back to life as a Christian doctor prayed. Muslims were being healed of incurable diseases and turning to Christ.

The Christians there were so excited and saying, 'We

can take this nation for God!' They believed God would do anything. Miracles were normal and numerous. The very atmosphere was charged with the Lord's presence.

The power of the tongue

Back in London, we crashed back down to earth. What a contrast – the city was so pessimistic. Everyone seemed to feel negative about the British, including the British themselves! This attitude had spilled over into the Church: 'It is so hard here, no one will ever get saved in this area', 'The devil has been chasing me all week', 'Whenever I talk about Jesus, people just don't want to listen', 'The Church is dying in the United Kingdom – it is such a hard slog'. The Bible says that the power of life and death are in the tongue, and here was the Church in London digging its own grave! My heart was downcast. I fasted and prayed, crying out to God.

After a few days, I heard God saying in an audible voice, 'Man of God, arise! Get up and go over this Jordan and take the people with you.' I looked around the room for this man of God', but there was no one there but me. Slowly it dawned on me that God was speaking to *me*. Would you believe it if God had said that to you?

How quick we are to believe the negative and how slow to believe the truth! God was prompting me to lead Christians out in evangelism to the local parish. Thoughts like 'You will be mocked and doors will be shut in your face' flooded my mind. But, at the same time, God seemed to be saying, 'There will be more doors open to you than you can cope with'. Sure enough, as we went out, doors were opened and people became Christians; others were healed and many came to church. The church grew to 500 people.

Slowly we began to speak differently. Instead of saying,

'It's too hard here', we would say, 'Nothing is too hard for the Lord'. 'The devil has been chasing me all week' changed to 'Surely goodness and mercy will follow me all the days of my life'. Those who had been saying 'Nothing ever happens when I speak' were now declaring, '. . . those who believe . . . will drive out demons; they will speak in new tongues . . . they will place their hands on sick people, and they will get well' (Mark 16:17–18).

Our beliefs, thoughts and actions changed, too. We went out into the area to preach the gospel as Jesus had commanded and he rewarded our efforts with a harvest. The Lord will bless you and reward you too as you take the initiative. Launch out in your area, expect great things from God, and great things will happen. You will not be disappointed!

Team evangelism

Evangelistic activity by a whole church or team is one of the tests of how well the leadership has heard from God and how seriously its members have sought to obey him. Hearing is one stage, but implementing God's strategy requires the utmost faithfulness at every subsequent stage. We must not work zealously for God with our own agenda, expecting him to bless our plans, because he will not!

Over the years I have experienced the blessing – and disappointment – of both faithful and flawed leadership in ambitious evangelistic projects. In talking about various outreaches, both here and overseas, I will be examining the importance of thorough preparation and *the right expectations* of what God will do through us, his witnesses.

It is a divine law that you reap what you sow! Whenever our church goes out, we believe that God is going to use

174

us to bring salvation to people with whom we speak. One German girl who worked with my team for a year on many fruitful outreaches said, 'I've done outreaches before where we went out and did our best, but this was the first time we actually believed that God was going to win people.'

No hard places – only worn-out methods

This statement may not be popular, but I believe that there are no hard places, only worn-out methods that have passed their 'sell-by date'.

Even in this visual age used to fast-moving action, I have proved repeatedly that normal people having some fun can present the gospel in a way that communicates at street level, sparks interest and provokes questions. The day of just giving out tracts, especially unintelligible ones, or one person preaching while others stand around looking scared, joyless or worn out, is over. Your method for your church may simply be what you have *always* done; however, the key is creativity and the boldness to open up your thinking to God. Every method that works comes from God.

Bringing the battle into the open

Many areas in our cities, towns and villages have been given over to the enemy, who rules these areas through materialism and blasphemy. Open-air evangelism is the way to make God known on the streets – not only to the people, but to the spiritual powers and authorities.

By enjoying God in the open air in the same way that we do in church, and leaving our safe church building to worship God, preach and declare the good news of Jesus, we start to change the spiritual atmosphere. The devil will flee because he is allergic both to praise and worship and the reading of God's Word.

Recently in Horsham, a number of churches grouped together to read the New Testament aloud from the Message Bible. People stopped to listen, but the real work was performed in the invisible realm, because the power of God's Word can soften the hardest ground. As God promised Joshua, so we believe that he gives us the ground we tread on: 'I will give you every place where you set your foot' (Josh. 1:3).

Prayer walks in twos, or in a larger group, are another powerful way of cleansing the spiritual atmosphere.

Street evangelism

Don't be surprised if you encounter opposition during your initial outreaches. At our Wembley church, our first attempt at outreach in a main square was interrupted by the arrival of the police – an angry caretaker had called them. The police could not understand why he was so angry, but we knew. We witnessed soundly to the police (it helped that we had a Christian police constable in our church!). We continued praying, and later the caretaker became a friend.

Resistance has always broken in the end, because we have kept going to the same place month after month, praising, worshipping and proclaiming God's loving character through music, drama and dance. Don't worry if your whole church cannot participate every month; even a committed few can make a marked difference.

Remember that the most memorable of outreaches can occur on the most ordinary of days! One exciting outreach started off in a very dull way. Every Friday night the small group of young people from Youth with a Mission gathered for prayer. It was hard, really tough, to continue praying when sleepiness threatened to envelop them, but they kept going, four to six of them, throughout the winter. They felt as if they were charging at an oak door with a battering ram, but they persisted until the door gave way.

Now imagine the scene in Nottingham's market square with about seven hundred people gathered on a sunny Saturday afternoon: punk rockers with spiked hair and chains mingling with the shoppers struggling with their plastic carrier bags; Satanists out in force; alcoholics slumped on the pavements amid bottles and broken glass; and a particularly violent, godless man threatening the YWAM team as they prepared to preach the gospel. What a setting for witnessing for Christ!

Twenty-five young people from Finland and Norway presented a forty-five minute drama, *The Toymaker*, supported by an equal number of 'YWAMers', mostly British, from YWAM's Summer of Service team. They performed on the square every day for a week. Between two hundred and seven hundred people, mostly non-Christians, watched enthralled. Even when the team leader preached for forty-five minutes, hardly anyone moved away. About one hundred people responded to the invitation to receive Christ that week. To God be the glory for ever and ever.

Why was this outreach so successful when so many are not? It is because of the point concerning prayer that I expounded a little earlier – that is, the ground had been thoroughly prepared:

1 There had been consistent prayer.
2 The media were informed and interviews were given to radio, television and newspapers.
3 The outreach was visual, full of colour and well performed by normal young people relating to others of their generation.

4 It was done well by individuals who had worked hard to get it right, even though they were amateurs.

5 Fifty is a large enough number to draw its own crowd, and people from other nations increase the curiosity value.

6 The place was right: the market square, where people were already congregating.

How to hold a successful open-air witness meeting

1 Length of programme It is better to keep the outreach to thirty or forty minutes of singing, drama, mime and testimony. You can repeat the same programme after an hour. You don't need professionals; God has a habit of anointing those who make themselves available. However, it *is* worth reading a book on drama and dance first.

2 Responsibilities Have a clear chain of command; one person should be the overall outreach leader, with others in charge of specific areas, such as the PA system, props, and supply of any tracts you are using. Make sure everyone understands these responsibilities, so that if someone wants the PA system quieter, they speak to the person responsible rather than attempting to alter it themselves.

3 Site Be selective, and choose a good site where people naturally congregate for a while. For instance, avoid car parks outside supermarkets. A good venue would be a market place, or where other major events are held, such as shopping precincts – bandstands and beaches can also be ideal. And don't forget, go and check out your venue before the outreach day.

4 Layout A workable format, which can be adapted, is

a horseshoe shape, with the open end to the crowd and the PA system and performers in the centre.

5 Keep alert You are an army, not a bunch of ramblers! Try to find a place where there is a wall behind you and appoint security people over the PA systems and musical equipment. Encourage the team to leave their valuables at home.

6 Praise and prayer You will, of course, have been praying for the outreach and the people you are going to meet for weeks beforehand. Now is the time to declare the character and nature of Christ and enforce his victory in that area through praise and intercessory prayer. You can start by walking around in twos, praying in agreement over key aspects of the outreach. Then gather together as a group. Have a praise leader in the centre leading in warfare, praise, prayer and declaration of the kingdom of God. Often this results in people stopping to see what is going on, but keep your focus on God. Do not stop to talk to them. This time is for the Lord and to bind enemy spirits.

7 Crowd pulling Attract a crowd by means of colourful clothes, painted faces and noise. A crowd attracts a crowd, so if you have a smaller church, attempt to work with others to bolster your numbers. Have your own 'rent-a-crowd' in front, praying quietly, cheering and clapping.

8 Perform professionally Keep one item following another rapidly: everyone must know exactly what they are doing beforehand. Don't pause between your song, drama, testimony or preaching (see the next point!).

9 Preaching versus personal witness Bear in mind that preaching does not often work well in this culture; usually it deters people from finding out more, and I only preach if I have a clear leading from the Holy Spirit to do so. Usually it is best to let the dramas and testimonies tell the message so that you can talk to people on a one-to-one basis afterwards, which I have found to be far more effective.

10 How to give a testimony in public If you are the one called on to give a testimony, remember that a detailed account on the street will often lose a crowd; be as short and as relevant as possible. Should there be a heckler in the crowd, who cannot be ignored, try to respond with humour. Some street evangelists are expert at giving such a funny reply that the crowd swings to their side, leaving the heckler out in the cold.

11 Mockers Mostly, mocking occurs within groups of people, so you are more likely to encounter it in an open-air outreach. I persevere with mockers, because it often becomes apparent that one person is interested. I focus on that person and address my remarks to them. The others will tend to move away after they have had their sport, leaving the interested one behind.

On other occasions, however, wisdom dictates to move away. Keep listening to the Holy Spirit's promptings. His promptings occur not when we theorise, but when we act. If you don't seem to hear God in a given situation, use your common sense! If we make the wrong decision, God will always overrule; in this way, he teaches us while on the job.

12 How to speak with spectators After the open-air event, or towards the end, position yourself beside people who have been listening and watching, ready to talk to them when it finishes. Don't all rush off after the people as one body! If you do, they will run away from you! Do you remember how you felt before you were a Christian, if you thought someone was trying to buttonhole you with their pet theory or sell you something? Be relaxed and friendly. If they walk off, you can go along with them and ask their opinion about what they have heard.

A good leading question after an outreach is, 'What did you think of the programme/drama/singing?' Never assume people know what the drama means. Most of the time, even when people respond to the question, it is clear that they did not understand the drama. At that point, I usually explain the true meaning. This is a great conversation opener, except when they say, 'It was rubbish!' In that instance, I respond by saying, 'I used to think just like you.' I laugh and tell them how I've changed in my thinking. Keep your sense of humour – if you get too serious, you will lose most people's interest. Conveying a serious message with a light touch is an acquired art, but it is essential, because the listener will swiftly detect any judgmental attitude. Let the Holy Spirit convict them of ungodliness, not you! The simplicity of the gospel message, given with love, will always open listeners' hearts and minds to God.

Listening to the Holy Spirit

You need to be listening to the Holy Spirit, and listening both to what the person is saying and *what they are not saying*. You can also tell a lot by body language; without becoming too psychologically oriented, you can usually tell that someone is receptive if their posture is relaxed – if their arms and legs are crossed, their minds are probably closed.

It is also worth nothing that the sexes differ as to how they prefer to be approached. Men tend to approach each other from the side to show that they are not being confrontational, whereas a woman is suspicious of anyone who sidles up beside her and prefers a stranger to stand in front of her.

People will know whether you love them or are just trying to 'gain another scalp' by the way you listen. *You* may know that their salvation is a burning issue of life and death, but only by listening to them first will you have earned the right to speak to them.

Once, after leading a French girl to Christ, she made a telling comment about evangelists: 'You listened to what I had to say, so I listened to what you had to say. Other Christians who spoke to me never listened.'

Supernatural help

When we witness to people, we can reach out and ask the Holy Spirit for revelation – just as Jesus had insight about the Samaritan woman at the well. Once I was confronted by a very sceptical young man. The gospel was like water bouncing off him, until the Lord revealed to me his personal life. I said, 'Your wife has walked out on you and you are broken-hearted.' He went very quiet. Tears filled his eyes, and now I had his attention.

The heart of all evangelism is love. Give people your undivided attention; don't look over their shoulder or let your eyes skim the crowd. You may feel inadequate or inarticulate, but if you are sincere about sharing the love of God with someone, 'love will cover a multitude of sins' and the person will begin to respect you for your attitude and demeanour.

While witnessing in the street, I often pray, 'Lord, make my heart more tender so that your love can flow out. Let this person I'm talking to be more important than my own needs and feelings of inadequacy, and as important to me as my own family.'

You may meet someone who seems to want to talk

for hours without a pause! This indicates that they have probably been living on their own; if they are elderly, you could be the first person they have spoken to for a week.

If someone refuses to be quiet, you may need to pray under your breath to stop an evil spirit from trying to prevent the person hearing the gospel. One warning: if you are working with a partner, make sure your partner is praying unobtrusively! I have actually seen people rolling their eyes and audibly praying in tongues while their partner is attempting to share their faith!

Another mistake is for one partner to interrupt the other, thinking they can say it better or say something different. It gives a very bad impression of Christian harmony if two people are fighting for the right to speak! By the time the two of them have finished lobbing their verbal gospel grenades back and forth, the poor interviewee almost needs healing from crossed eyes! So you need to agree that you will take it in turns for one person only to speak while the other prays silently.

This need not be a hard-and-fast rule; one person may feel the other has something useful to contribute, so he can stop while the other speaks for a few moments; it might be a particular testimony that would be relevant to the interviewee. But remember that you are not competing; you are a team. Even if you are very experienced, and know you could do the job better than your less experienced partner, refrain from jumping in and stick to your previous arrangements, supporting them in prayer. Remember that a person must be free to fail; this is part of a leader's delegation.

Potential pitfalls to avoid

1 Don't place a lone speaker or small group in an area

where they have to shout to make themselves heard above traffic noise.

2 Do not use religious 'jargon' – this is another opportunity to test the street credibility of your testimony! Ask a spectator what they thought of 'the experience which that person described', rather than 'the testimony that was shared'. Any statements like 'Are you saved?' or 'Are you washed in the blood?' will not mean anything to a non-believer. (Refer to Chapter 3 for more on Christian jargon.)

3 Avoid wearing clothes that make you look different from everyone else. A group of men in suits and ties will make you look like Mormons. Loosen up, and enhance your 'street cred' by wearing comfortable, practical clothes.

Running a mission overseas

Imagine a large, gloomy square in Copenhagen, filled with rebellious local people and riot police with batons charging among them. Blood was spilled and both sides were badly injured. It took the police months to calm the resultant outrage.

Several months later, this was the venue for four weeks of outreach planned by a local church. They invited me, and our team of fifty people training with YWAM in England, to lead it. Clearly, they were expecting great things from our visit – so were we. Why, then, were we seeing so small a response to the gospel? We were disappointed that only a few of the church people came out with us on the streets. Normally, we would expect to work together *with* the church – not to do the work for them! After three weeks, we were physically and emotionally exhausted.

There were several reasons for the failure of the first three weeks. One was the lack of preparation in prayer by the church, which meant that the square where the riot took place still had an ugly atmosphere. On one occasion, when I leaned over towards a large, well-built man and started speaking to him about the love of God, his bitterness was evident.

'They baton-charged us,' he blurted out. 'Three of them beat me up and worked me over with their batons.' He pointed to a long, ugly scar running down his head and face. 'Then the judge gave me six months in jail!' Turning his head, he spat expressively. 'It happened right here in this square.'

Listening to him, I was conscious of darkness spreading over the people in the square. I talked with the man for about twenty minutes until the groups of Christian students began to gather, preparing to portray the love of God in song, mime, dance and testimony.

Suddenly a wild woman burst into the square and threatened to punch anyone who said the wrong thing. Gently, we tried to ease her away and she eventually went, but only after she had pushed one of the men to the ground and said words over him that could only have been inspired by a demon. It was tough-going as the Christian group began to sing and dance; evil forces were opposing us. 'Keep going,' I thought, 'Keep praying until the opposition breaks.'

From the corner of my eye, I saw a young member of the group approach the man I had spoken to earlier. 'That's enough!' the man snapped, pointing in my direction. The youngster moved quickly away. As the performance progressed, the wild woman appeared again, trying to disrupt the watching children.

It was then that something amazing happened. About six of the small children began to testify and sing and, as they did, the power of God came upon the woman and thrust her right out of the square. Later she tried to return, but could not get beyond an invisible barrier at the edge of the area. We later found out that the people in that place loved the woman and would have attacked us if we had tried to be forceful with her in any way. After that the presence of God increased, and later that night, in the Labour Club overlooking the square, three people became Christians.

Heaven was rejoicing; light had penetrated the darkness and it had been worth all the struggle and spiritual warfare.

The outreach in Copenhagen was the most difficult I had ever led. Each square seemed to be full of drunks who verbally threatened us; some raised their fists and others menaced us with bottles. The same 'wild woman' jumped on me, hanging round my neck as I instructed team members. I remembered God's promise to Paul the apostle, 'Do not be afraid; keep on speaking, do not be silent. For I am with you, and no-one is going to attack and harm you, because I have many people in this city' (Acts 18:9–10).

On the Sunday of the final week the church met together. They were disappointed, too. They had been expecting hundreds to be saved, but had done little to help. Seeing the state we were in, they rose up as one and prayed for us, repenting with tears for their absence on the outreach and for their lack of support for us.

The last week was completely different. The church members were out in force with us, sharing testimonies on the streets. It was the glorious Church in action. The Holy Spirit flowed and many people received Christ.

We had been disappointed because our expectations had been different and unrealistic. The local church was expecting us to do all the work for them and to go out and reach hundreds of people for Christ. We were expecting the church to pray and work with us and, knowing the area better than we did, to have a realistic goal for harvest. Many hurts and misunderstandings can be prevented if church and visiting teams get together before an outreach or mission and share their hopes, methods of approach and commitment to the project.

Questions for the visiting team

• Has the church evangelised the area before? In Copenhagen the answer was no. There will be a poor harvest without first sowing the seeds of preaching, prayer, fasting, evangelism, friendship and love.

• Has the church prayed for the mission? When evangelist Billy Graham is invited to a city, he asks them how long they have been praying. If the answer is a year, he will say, 'Pray for another year and then I will come.' He gets results!

• Do the people in the church really want the mission, and are they prepared to make sacrifices and participate?

Questions for the church being visited by an outreach team

• What is the spiritual maturity of the visiting team? And the level of spiritual maturity in your church? Is the maturity, and mix of maturity, appropriate to the people and situations they will encounter?

• Have any members of the visiting team preached in church before? If so, how experienced is/are the preacher (s), and what results do they get? You would be a brave (or, probably, foolish) pastor to let a novice preacher loose on your people!

• Has the visiting team been involved with open-air missions or door-to-door work before? Were they successful?

• Do their team members have counselling skills, and or are they gifted in healing?

• Are the team members strong in their faith, giving prayer a high priority, or are they tired and discouraged, or struggling through a lack of finance?

The answers to these questions will help to set realistic goals, expectations and strategy as church and team wait on God together to plan the outreach. Team members will differ in their maturity level, but almost all must have a commitment and zeal to win the lost to Christ which can be channelled by church and team leaders working together.

Immature teams need a daily programme of teaching, intercession and spending time together. The inexperienced can then be used in door-to-door evangelism, and work with a more experienced person in open-air witness and in singing, mime, dance or giving a testimony.

A more experienced team can train and encourage the local church in evangelism. Outreach then becomes a shared venture, and the church is left to continue evangelising their area with confidence when the team has left.

An example of this type of training occurred unexpectedly when Joyce and I took a mature team of YWAM staff members to south-east Asia for five months. What happened next showed us how a mature, proven team can work creatively, responding to God's strategy.

In the Philippines, our programme in the university was suddenly cancelled. We prayed, 'Father, what do you want us to do?' The answer came in many different ways, through Scriptures, prophecies and words of knowledge, until we knew that God was telling us: 'Go to the mountains in the north of Manila, to the city of Bagio, to minister to the tribal people there.'

'But we already have three teams up here,' the YWAM base leader said. 'How experienced are you as a team?'

I replied, 'They're all YWAM staff with a fair amount of experience.'

'OK, come up and take over the church,' he replied gratefully.

It transpired that the pastor of this young church, and his wife and family, had all caught hepatitis and were convalescing at their home in Canada. For a month, our team acted as stop-gaps, taking over all kinds of ministry. People were converted and healed, and those who had lost their faith were restored, as we allowed God to use our maturity and experience in this unexpected situation until the local ministry returned to normal.

What kind of team?

Make sure that your aim is clear. Do you want an intercession team? Then ask for one. YWAM has specialist teams, but do not expect an evangelistic team to spend weeks in intercession or a children's team to work mainly with adults.

Pray and think through your aims, then aim for the target. Do you want a team to reach out primarily to children, youth, men only, or women? Do you want a music group, worship or drama team, people to encourage your members in missionary outreach?

When, as a church or as a team, we were sure of God's

will in our work, no one was ever disappointed with the results because we knew it was of God and we were able to see wonderful results.

Right attitudes in visiting teams

Visiting teams are sometimes considered to be 'the cream' of their own ministry or church, but their zeal may not match that of every member of their host church.

If a team does not come in with the right attitude, its members are in danger of judging the leaders of the church they are supposed to serve. Not all teams are like this, of course, but many are; if this is the case, the team needs teaching on how to serve and bless the host church.

Pride will create barriers between people, but a humble, loving servant heart opens doors and lays the foundation for a good working relationship with those they have come to help. I always teach my teams not to despise menial tasks; you should always be ready to put out chairs, make coffee, work the PA equipment, pray (of course!), go out door-to-door visiting, and deliver leaflets. When you have proved faithful in these activities, you will be entrusted with a larger ministry.

Submitting to leadership

Most teams face challenges when submitting to unfamiliar leadership. If all leaders were perfect, there would be no problems, but of course most are not! If there are problems, don't grumble or sulk; instead, talk things through. Be submissive and humble, and God himself will exalt you in his time. If there is a really serious problem, seek help from someone higher up in the same organisation. Most problems, though, arise from differences in personalities or methods and, as such, can usually be worked through.

Tips for host churches

Sometimes churches want visiting teams to work until the members drop, but a team will work better if it has its own needs met. If you receive a team in your area, consider what you can give, as well as what you expect to receive. Have the team members been on the road for weeks? Do they need encouragement, ministry or prayer? Would they benefit from fun times or a rest day to refresh them, or are they keen to get on with the job?

On arriving in one particular country, I was told that we would be expected to work non-stop and to give everything we had. I intimated that the team would need a day off every week. The organiser looked horrified, but I stood my ground and we had our days off!

Team leader's responsibilities

The team leader should cater for all three areas of his team's lives – spirit, soul and body. Make sure you have some fun times as well as hard work. Physical exercise and social interaction have their place alongside prayer, fasting and Bible study. Stretch your minds with cultural research about the people in the area. If they speak a different language, learn some words and try them out.

May God bless you, and have fun on your next outreach!

191

SUMMARY

For successful outdoor evangelism, take note of the following points:

• Make thorough preparation through prayer, good publicity, hard work, sufficient numbers, the right place.

• Practise giving your own testimony. Write it down so you can give it in three minutes.

• False expectations lead to disappointment. Right expectations bring joy and encouragement.

• Meditate on 1 Corinthians 12:12–30. Ask yourself, 'Am I confident as part of a team? What gifts can I bring to a team ministry?'

FOR GROUP DISCUSSION

Aim of the chapter
By the end of the meeting, participants will:

1 Understand better the need for realistic expectations in evangelism, and the importance of unity and fellowship in the body of Christ if we are to see fruit in mission.

2 Have considered how they might be involved as a team or church in open-air evangelism and asked God to show them specific talents or testimonies to be used on the street.

3 Have thought through the key issues involved in going on a mission to a church, and receiving an evangelistic mission at their church.

Key Scriptures
Study the following Scriptures:

1 *Jeremiah 29:11*: 'For I know the plans I have for you,' declares the LORD, 'plans to prosper you and not to harm you, plans to give you hope and a future.'

2 *2 Corinthians 6:1*: As God's fellow-workers we urge you not to receive God's grace in vain.

3 *1 Corinthians 3:9:* For we are God's fellow-workers; you are God's field, God's building.

Action/group participation
Divide the group into two. One half of the group is to represent the elders of the church who are expecting a visiting mission team for two weeks; the other half is to represent the leaders of a visiting mission team. In each group, and without any collaboration between the groups, talk through and write down the answers to the following questions:

1 What do you expect to achieve from this mission? (Include the number of new converts you expect to make.)

2 What do you realistically expect the team/church to provide in terms of numbers of people, talents and giftings, number of hours of work (prayer, witnessing, ministry, teaching, counselling, hospitality, time off, etc.) each day?

3 Draw up an outline plan for the two-week mission.

4 What communication structure(s) between team and church do you think you need before, during and after the mission?

5 What preparation for the mission are you expecting your own group, and the other group, to make?

Now appoint two members of each group to perform a

role-play in which they share your mutual expectations and iron out differences. Note the differences in people's expectations and see if the ease or difficulty you have in ironing out these differences surprises you.

It will make the role-playing more fun and helpful if it is realistic. (A visiting team that asks for round-the-clock intercessory and spiritual warfare cover from a small traditional church will *not* find their request greeted by the church leaders with 'Sure. No problem'!) At the end of the meeting, draw up (as far as is possible in the time) an agreed programme for the two weeks.

Come together as a group and discuss what lessons you have learned from this exercise.

Suggestions for group leaders
• Role-playing is both fun and daunting. Stay light-hearted and encourage people to have fun. It isn't a contest in acting skill. Light-hearted teasing (for example, letting someone 'take off' a local church leader) is fine so long as it comes out of a clean heart, but stop it right away if it threatens to get out of hand.

• If most of the group come from one church, little briefing will be necessary. If the group is made up of people from different churches, you will need to prepare a scene-setting briefing about the church that is being role-played (you may want to do this anyway for the 'visiting team'). But don't give everything away by, in effect, telling the group what their expectations are going to be.

• You will need to plan the timetable for the exercise carefully and make sure that the groups stick to it. If they don't, you'll find that you haven't managed to do half what you hoped to do.

• Be realistic – in this exercise we are not looking for

perfection, but for models that work. Theory only has a place if it can be worked out in practice. If at all possible, try to work some of the ideas out with a visiting team, then come back as a group, at a later date, to evaluate how well their ideas worked.

10

MORE POWER TO YOU

'I tell you the truth, anyone who has faith in me will
do what I have been doing. He will do even greater
things than these, because I am going to the Father'
(John 14:12).

Signs and wonders are God's 'calling card'

Signs and wonders are God's 'calling card'. Jesus, the
apostles and other believers had tremendous results through
miracles, deliverances and healings. Crowds followed
Jesus because they saw people healed and miracles performed, and they stayed to hear his teaching. The Bible
also tells us that when Peter visited Lydda and Aeneas
was healed of paralysis, all 'those who lived in Lydda
and Sharon saw him and turned to the Lord' (Acts 9:35).
Soon afterwards, Tabitha was raised from the dead in
Joppa, and many in that town 'believed in the Lord'
(Acts 9:36–43).

Jesus commanded us to heal the sick and cast out
demons. Certainly this gets people's attention. In fact,
according to author Peter Wagner, statistics show that this
is a major factor in church growth today. I believe that
we are in a new era where ordinary believers are seeing
miracles. Jesus said, 'Those who have faith in me . . .';

this means *every* believer. Jesus also said that a believer will do the same works that he himself did. What did Jesus do? He healed the sick, raised the dead, cleansed lepers and cast out demons. Mark 16 says that those who believe will lay hands on the sick and they shall recover.

I have seen the power of God openly displayed to the sceptic and the uninterested in England, the Philippines, Malaysia and Kenya. In Kenya, God stopped the monsoon rains so people could attend our gospel campaign meeting. In Uganda, the instant healing of a deaf, dumb and mentally disturbed boy caused a great stir in his village, and many were then converted.

These events communicated the nature and love of God to people of other languages and culture in a way that mere words could not express. The supernatural power of God can make a way for the gospel of Christ to be proclaimed and received.

While on a ministry trip to the Philippines, a non-Christian knocked on our door. This woman was a tribal Philippino; I was English. We struggled with broken English, but our communication and understanding was almost nil. The YWAM team and I decided to pray for her. After we laid hands on her she jerked, jumped and shrieked, and then began running around the front room shouting at the top of her voice.

Later, amid the excitement, we discovered that the woman had been instantly healed of three major incurable diseases. A member of our team had no difficulty in leading the woman to Christ after her miraculous recovery.

A young doctor in India was dying of kidney failure. His fellow doctors had done everything medically possible to save their friend but, in spite of that, he had been sent home to die. He had called upon his gods to heal him, but to no avail.

One day, in desperation, he prayed, 'Jesus, if you are

there, come and heal me and I will serve you for the rest of my life.' Suddenly, his whole body was engulfed with a fiery heat that passed through him. He was completely healed. I had the privilege then to preach in his house at a celebration to tell neighbours, friends, relatives and others of God's great miracle; many of these people responded to Christ.

The miraculous power of God can bend the hardest will. At one time, I had no ready answer for Mark, a young man from Mauritius living in east London. He was a Communist, and a wild young man running with an equally wild gang; trouble and fights were common occurrences. Mark seemed totally godless and unreachable.

Mark's mother, Mrs Jones, had an incurable disease that had caused haemorrhaging and ensuing weakness for many years. Unknown to Mrs Jones, her wayward son had made an agreement with the God he did not believe in. 'Heal my mum and I'll believe in you,' he had told the Lord. When Nicholas Rivett-Carnac and I laid hands on Mrs Jones and commanded her healing, the bleeding stopped instantly. A Christian then led Mark to the Lord and, as a result of that one miracle, this whole, large family turned to Christ. Mark is now a pastor in a London-based church.

Of course, not all who are healed turn to Christ. In the Bible, sadly, there are stories where those who are healed refuse to recognise the healer. Those people are in the minority, thankfully; the majority follow Christ after witnessing miracles and wonders.

While I was witnessing door to door in south London, a young mother showed me her baby, who had a huge tumour. She was distressed at what the doctors had told her and at what they were planning to do. I asked the young woman if I could pray for her baby, explaining that she had nothing to lose and, although embarrassed, she agreed. The tumour disappeared right before our startled eyes. We both gulped and looked at each other – it was gone! I later looked across the rows of chairs in church and saw mother and baby sitting in our Sunday service for the first time. God's 'calling card' is better than any humanistic method, programme or gimmick!

Why do we not use God's 'calling card' more often?

I have observed that Christians copy and follow the leadership given to them; in fact, they rarely go beyond it. It should be normal for every church member to heal the sick and perform miracles. If you are a church leader, you are called to model and lead your people into the supernatural power of God. There is anointing by association – faith is caught!

In the Philippines, a thousand-strong congregation did exactly what their pastor taught and showed them. Every week, deaf, blind and crippled people were healed in the services. Every day, the young believers prayed for others to receive the same miracles and healings that they themselves had received – and they did.

Are you a believer? If so, such miracles are also your heritage. We have been robbed of our heritage both by leaving the 'power gifts' to the one-man 'super-shows' and also because of our own doubts and wrong teaching. But God's Word promises that believers will do even greater works than the ones that were accomplished in the life of Jesus (John 14:12).

Paul says in 1 Corinthians 12:1, 'Now about spiritual gifts, brothers, I do not want you to be ignorant.' So the very first step to using God's gifts is to stop being ignorant and to become informed. Doing an open-hearted study of the Scriptures concerning these gifts is essential in this. The working of miracles is a *gift*. It is not based

199

on maturity or merit, but upon the generosity of the One who gives freely. A gift is not earned, but received with joyful thanks.

Your divine tool-kit

If a plumber, called to mend a leaky sink, arrived without his tool-kit and tried to undo a nut with his fingers, what would you think of him? I suspect you would think that either he was not a real plumber, or that he was not a very good one.

This is like a Christian who tries to live the Christian life without his God-given tool-kit – the nine gifts of the Holy Spirit (1 Cor. 12:7–10). These manifestations are potentially available for *every* believer, so take your tool-kit and use it! Without these gifts of grace, a Christian will constantly struggle and usually fail, because they are left exposed in the face of sickness and demons.

However, Jesus said, 'I have given you authority to trample on snakes and scorpions and to overcome all the power of the enemy; nothing will harm you' (Luke 10:19). Do you believe him? An Argentinian pastor related how he had been begging God for more authority over evil spirits. God spoke into his heart: 'I have already given you the authority; now use it.'

The pastor took God at his word and great deliverances and miracles began to happen. Like this pastor, we too must believe that we have authority over snakes, scorpions and all the power of the enemy. I often ask, 'If Jesus has given you all the authority over the enemy, how much power does that leave the enemy?'

We may not have a problem believing that demons are under Jesus's feet, but under mine? That's different! But since we are in Christ, placed into Jesus himself, what is under his feet is also under ours. We have been placed together with Jesus in the heavenly places, far above all the enemy's principalities and powers (Eph. 1:3, 2:6). It has been said that if you have a message for Satan, you should write it on the sole of your foot!

There are so many who make the enemy seem more powerful than he is, in statements like, 'You are in front-line ministry, therefore you are bound to be attacked.' The Bible says that I am blessed and protected by God when I am in his will. Those in danger are those who run ahead of God or lag behind him. I have learned that if you expect a great fight, that's what you will get. Expect to be harmed, and sometimes that happens too.

Let's renew our minds by thinking differently: 'I have been given authority and demons are under my feet.' As we believe *and act upon* the Word of God, the gifts of the Holy Spirit will flow through us to set the captives free, as promised to us in Isaiah 61:1: 'The Spirit of the Sovereign LORD is on me, because the LORD has anointed me to preach good news to the poor. He has sent me to bind up the broken-hearted, to proclaim freedom for the captives and release from darkness for the prisoners . . .'

Where do we find the gifts of the Holy Spirit? In the Holy Spirit himself. Where does the Holy Spirit live? In us – so the gifts live in us too! The apostle Paul says, in 1 Corinthians 14:1, 'Follow the way of love and eagerly desire spiritual gifts, especially the gift of prophecy.'

When I teach about spiritual gifts, I often ask people how many of them want to receive them. It always amazes me to see that some do not have this desire. If you love people, you will want to see them saved and healed, and you will need your tool-kit to do the job properly.

A well-known evangelist was preaching to 50,000 people in south India. His ministry was full of miracles and he was challenging the Indian Christians to seek God, fast, pray, and earnestly and persistently desire the nine gifts of the Holy Spirit. Among those present was a young banker, who listened and responded to this challenge. For three years, early in the morning and after work, he would be on his knees in earnest prayer, seeking the gift of healing. At the end of three years, his healing and miracle ministry began. Crowds of 250,000 amassed to hear the gospel. This man was enabled by God to call the sufferers by name, tell them their doctors' names, their conditions and medication, and then he would explain exactly how God was healing them at that moment. It all began with a persistent desire, and perseverance in prayer until God answered.

One minister asked a group of pastors, 'How badly do you want the gifts?' One of the pastors laid on his face calling to God, and God spoke to him: 'The gifts in the Church of America are waning. I want them to increase, not decrease!' Miracles are there all the time for every church and every believer, not only for Sundays at church. The 'calling card' of God must be used at the door, in the street and in the market-place. Do not say, 'It can't happen here', because it *is* happening here – and it will increase. Will you be a part of it? How badly do you desire and want these gifts? Desire them for your own ministry. Earnestly desire all nine gifts, and pray persistently for them to be manifested in the churches.

Some Christians are intense. They try so hard that they block the flow of God's Spirit, but this flow has nothing to do with human endeavour. The Holy Spirit gives the gifts to whom he wills, when he wills. Relax. All you have to do is persistently desire his gifts and ask him to use the gifts through you as he wills so you can fulfil your gifting and calling on earth. After you have read the following brief definitions of the gifts of the Spirit, spend time worshipping and waiting upon God and he will do the rest.

Gifts of the Spirit

Read 1 Corinthians 12:8–11:

> To one there is given through the Spirit the message of wisdom, to another the message of knowledge by means of the same Spirit, to another faith by the same Spirit, to another gifts of healing by that one Spirit, to another miraculous powers, to another prophecy, to another distinguishing between spirits, to another speaking in different kinds of tongues, and to still another the interpretation of tongues. All these are the work of one and the same Spirit, and he gives them to each one, just as he determines.

We have already mentioned words of knowledge; they will come into your head just when you need them in order to break down resistance to the gospel. Now I want to look at the other gifts.

The gift of tongues Hundreds of Christians have received this gift through our ministry. Here is a typical dialogue:
'Have you received the baptism of the Holy Spirit?'
'No.'
'Have you asked God for this experience?'
'Yes.'
'How do you know you haven't received it?'
'I can't speak in tongues. In fact, I've been begging God for it for years.'
'God never holds out on those who ask. He says in Luke 11:9–13: "How much more will your Father in

heaven give the Holy Spirit to those who ask him!"
Rather than beg, because you're not a beggar, why not
put another biblical principle into practice and *believe
you have received what you asked for*. Start thanking
God instead.'

Once people relax into gratitude, the gift of tongues
quickly follows!

The gift of distinguishing (discerning) of spirits Many
believers are already using this gift without giving God
the credit! It is seen in the way they 'sense' atmospheres
– the presence of the Holy Spirit or ungodly spirits – or
recognise when a prophecy or spiritual manifestation is of
God. Frequently people will say, 'That prophecy sounded
good, but here inside it didn't feel right.'

And they are absolutely right. This gift is valuable
in prayer. For example, when you are praying for your
neighbourhood, the Holy Spirit may show you that evil
spirits, or perhaps angels, are present.

The gift of working of miracles Most Christians in
the West put miracles out of reach. We tend to believe
that God will grant us more of his gifts and power as
we mature spiritually.

This, of course, is a fallacy. I have heard new Christians
in south-east Asia reporting the miraculous regularly. The
same believers asked me for guidance on how to grow
in God. I too experienced the same working of miracles
when I was a new Christian with regard to my own
problems and needs.

Once we emerge from this false thinking, we can
begin to see a return to the 'normal Christianity' seen
in Acts, and at other times of revival in history. At one
of our Faith Camps, the senior pastor remarked on the
number of miracles. My reaction was, 'At last – normal
Christianity.'

The gift of faith Have you ever prayed for someone or something, and at a certain point felt your doubt evaporate because you had received your answer from God?

That is the gift of faith in action; it is another gift that people are operating unconsciously! After praying, perhaps for years, to see the salvation of a loved one, the healing of the sick, or the provision of something you needed, there came a point when something clicked in your spirit and you could say with assurance, 'I have the answer. God has done it.'

This wonderful gift is often accompanied by gifts of healing and the working of miracles; we call them 'the power gifts'.

The gift of prophecy Paul exhorts us to desire the gift of prophecy especially (1 Cor. 14:2). He knew that its true purpose, as seen throughout the Bible, is not necessarily a string of predictions about someone's future! Rather it is to 'edify' or build up believers – to encourage, exhort and comfort them. Have you met anyone in church lately who needed encouragement and comfort? Ask God for the gift of prophecy; like all the gifts, it is to benefit others. Let's summarise our approach to the gifts of the Spirit:

1 Be informed.
2 Desire the spiritual gifts.
3 Thank God that the gifts are already within you.
4 Reach out in love, and the Holy Spirit will manifest his great gifts to those who need them.

What is the best gift? The answer is the one that is needed at the time. If someone needs healing, it is the healing gift imparted to the sick person that will drive out sickness (1 Cor. 14:2).

Raised from the dead

My good friend, Victor Okiegie, was walking down Brixton Road in south London when a lady fell off the bus, hitting the ground with a terrible thud. Victor rushed to her only to find that she was dead; she had no pulse or sign of breathing, and she was turning blue. 'Lord, what should I do?' he enquired. 'Command her to come back to life,' the Lord replied. By this time, a large crowd had gathered, but Victor boldly commanded the lady to live. After some time had passed, she opened her eyes and sat up. She was presented alive to her family, all of whom received Jesus as their Saviour, as did the lady herself. It happened on the streets of Brixton, and it will happen right where you are. God is raising up an end-time army. This is for normal believers, for the whole body of Christ, and not just for 'one-man super shows'. The world will receive God's 'calling card'.

Persecution

Be prepared, however, for persecution and face it with wisdom. Jesus was anointed with the wisdom of God. We could say, 'Yes, but that is Jesus, not lil' ol' me.' But Jesus was totally dependent on the Holy Spirit, just as we are! 1 John 2:6 states, 'who ever claims to live in him must walk as Jesus did.' When persecution arises – and it will – our dependence upon the Holy Spirit for wisdom will be critical. Jesus was opposed almost everywhere he went. The more we move in power, the more confrontation we will experience. The Word says we are to walk as he walked. May God bless you as you respond to take up this great challenge.

This is my prayer for those who read this book: I pray

that God will raise up an army through you all; I ask for the anointing to be released upon you to see miracles, salvation, signs and wonders multiplied in your daily lives, in the name of Jesus.

Now respond to this prayer: 'Father, in Jesus's name, I now receive power to fulfil your Word. I receive a multiplication* of your gifts in my life now, in Jesus's name. Amen.'

FOR MEDITATION AND PRAYER

Mark 16:15–18; Luke 9:1–2; Luke 10:1–9; Acts 4:29–31.

FOR GROUP DISCUSSION

Aim of the chapter
By the end of the meeting, participants will:

1 Know more about the gifts of the Spirit and believe that these gifts are for them *today*.

2 Be baptised in the Spirit if they weren't before, and/or understand how to be released in the use of the gifts.

3 Believe that their role as witnesses will be transformed when they start to move in supernatural giftings.

Key Scriptures
Read and meditate on the following Scriptures, underlining or making a note of verses that particularly speak to you:

---

* 'Multiplication' is seen as a result of God's blessing throughout the Bible, from the Garden of Eden to the Abrahamic Covenant (Gen. 28:3), to the parables of Jesus. The kingdom of God is always associated with growth and multiplication (for example, the parable of the sower), whereas Satan's activities only bring loss, destruction and death. Other 'multiplication' references are: Exodus 7:3; 2 Corinthians 9:10; Acts 9:31 and 12:24.

1 *Matthew 28:18–19; Mark 16:15–18; Luke 9:1–2; Luke 10:1–9; Acts 4:29–31; Acts 9: 32–43; Acts 19:1–6; 1 Corinthians 12:1, 4–11; 1 Corinthians 14:1.*

2 *Read Luke 11:9–13.* Ask yourself, and answer, the following questions from this passage:
  (a) What will happen when I ask?
  (b) What will happen when I seek?
  (c) Does 'everyone' include me?
  (d) What will God do if I ask him for baptism in the Holy Spirit *now*?
  (e) What will God do if I ask him for the gifts of the Spirit *now*?

Group participation
Respond individually and as a group (as appropriate) to the following questions/prompting:

1 What in this chapter, and the Scripture passages mentioned, has moved you most? Would you like your ministry to show these giftings? Which gifts do you think God wants you to have and be able to use now? Which gifts do you want to move in most urgently?

2 Are you baptised in the Holy Spirit and manifesting one or more of the supernatural gifts listed in 1 Corinthians 12? If not, do you want to be? If you do, ask the group leader what you should do to be baptised in the Holy Spirit.

3 What would be the impact in your church and locality if *every* member of your church was regularly demonstrating the spiritual gifts, just as the early Church was?

4 Are you willing to pay the price of being a powerful Christian witness – in terms of prayer and fasting, persecution and loss of privacy as many seek God and his help through you? If you are (and even if you aren't, for that matter!), what can you do about it *today*?

Prayer

Pray as a group and individually (as appropriate) the following prayers:

1 For church leaders that they may prove worthy models of Christ-like ministry for their people to grow towards and emulate.

2 For protection from discouragement and persecution for those moving in these gifts. And for perseverance in prayer and seeking a Christ-like lifestyle for those looking for a greater anointing in power ministry.

3 For a release of power gifts in every person in the group and in the churches in your locality.

Action

1 Those group members who do use one or more of the gifts of the Spirit should give their testimony (either to their neighbour or to the whole group if it is small) as to how the Lord has used them to build his Church and bless his people.

2 After praying for baptism in the Spirit for every group member who wants to receive this gift, and for the release of all the gifts of the Spirit, spend time allowing each other to practise what they have received, especially tongues. Ask everyone who has been prayed for what happened when they prayed to receive baptism in the Holy Spirit.

Suggestions for group leaders

• Remember that every gift from God is a 'grace gift'; we can't *earn* spiritual gifts. Therefore someone who moves strongly in these gifts is not 'superior' to another who still hasn't manifested the same gifts.

  Every gift is given and used to draw attention and glory to the giver – Jesus – not to the recipient or user of the gift. All we have to do is seek the gift by asking for it with humble and obedient hearts, believing God will give it, and being willing to use the gifts he gives as he directs.

Prepare yourself to lead the group into a release of the Spirit in its members' lives and ministries. If you feel inadequate for the task, ask someone to help you who is more fluent in the gifts of the Spirit.

The enemy will do all he can to discourage you from releasing the group into these giftings. He knows how powerfully the group will damage his kingdom after this meeting. *For the kingdom's sake, please do not listen to him, however persuasive or bullying he becomes.*

• Look at next week's meeting programme. If the group is large, you may want to split the meeting over two weeks. In the first week do everything planned except letting each person preach their gospel message. Then follow this with a preaching meeting the following week.

• If appropriate, given the size of your group, warn the group that they need to come prepared to give a three-minute gospel message at the next meeting. They need to re-read Chapter 3, 'The Message', before they prepare what they are going to say. Encourage *everyone* to look forward to doing this. It's what the course has been all about!

11

HAVE PLANES, WILL TRAVEL

Jesus said, 'Therefore go and make disciples of all nations
. . .' (Matt. 28:19). 'Nations' here means 'people groups'
who have their own language, dialect, culture, customs
and history. Often there are many such groups within
a political nation, and many who still do not have the
Bible in their own languages. The Scriptures are full
of examples of people who were sent by God as his
messengers to different nations.

If we claim to know him, then we must obey him and
go! Hudson Taylor was a famous missionary to China. One
of his Chinese converts once asked, 'How long has the
gospel been known in England?' 'Oh, hundreds of years,'
he replied. With tears streaming down his face, the new
convert said, 'My father and grandfathers were seekers after
truth. Why didn't someone come from England earlier?'

Is your church aware of the need to reach these
unreached groups? Seek to create this awareness. How
much of your manpower and resources are used to fulfil
Jesus's command to 'make disciples of *all* nations' – in
other words, *all* people groups?

Every church should have a missionary department,
and every Christian should consider long- or short-term
missions. A short-term mission has the effect of opening
the eyes of the missionary to new people, and to different
cultures and beliefs.

In St Mark's Church, Kennington, London, forty missionaries were sent out to the mission field. This fell short of my target (10 per cent of church members), as the church was 500-strong. How many of your church members are out on short-/long-term missions?

While I recommend short-term missions and have seen lives changed in many of those who have participated, this is not seen as a substitute for God's strategy of long-term missions, although many people who go on short mission trips become so gripped with the vision that they become long-term missionaries later on.

Make it your priority to try to find out from the Lord exactly what he requires of you. Seek to motivate, and go with, your own church. There are so many opportunities world-wide! There is enough for everyone to do before the return of Christ.

True state of church giving

How much of your church finances are being used for short- and long-term missionary work? Some years ago I was staggered by some statistics about church finances: 95 per cent of the church budget was being spent on the running of the church, with 4.5 per cent on missions, and 0.5 per cent to unreached people groups (e.g. through Scripture translation).

Can you hear the cry of the people calling out to you as they plunge into a Christless eternity? Keith Green sang a song called 'Jesus commands us to go'. He said that you have to go unless you have a call to stay!

A YWAM leader from Canada once told me they had purchased a plane and a train for gospel work. I was amazed. I am missions-minded, but this thinking was BIG! A short time ago, another leader said that they wanted to charter a jumbo jet to take the whole church of 600 people on a short-term mission. He stated that the mould of religious thinking in the land needed to be broken.

The reason why God blesses a country is so that its people may go and bless other people groups. As Scripture says, 'From everyone who has been given much, much will be demanded' (Luke 12:48).

While in Singapore on a mission trip, I had the privilege of addressing the bishop and clergy from the Anglican churches there. Their unity is amazing. God has visited this small island in a very special way from the late 1970s onwards and almost all sections of the community have been affected by the gospel.

As I preached that day, I felt a prophetic utterance rising from deep within me, stemming from God's words to Abraham, 'I will bless you so that you can be a blessing to many nations' (Paraphrase of Gen. 12:2–3).

'Singapore has been blessed economically, socially and spiritually,' I told the bishop and clergy. 'Are you prepared to take this blessing to the four corners of the world, especially to Asia? Are you willing to bless India, the Philippines, Indonesia and other lands with gospel teams and practical skills and to take this two-handed gospel to the whole of Asia?' Singapore has started to do this, but only in a small way compared to the richness that God has bestowed on it. In another meeting, I preached on the call to missions and asked, 'Would you be willing to go wherever the Lord sends you?' Only a handful of people stood to signify their willingness. I was not asking them to go, but only to be available. Clearly most of them were not. God's purpose is to spread his Word to the nations (people groups). Abraham was blessed by God to be a blessing to the nations. Jesus's urgent command was for the gospel to be preached to every people group. Then the end would come.

The Jews struggled with a similar problem to that of

the people we met in Singapore. The outer court in the temple was the place where the Gentiles were supposed to hear about God. The Jews failed to proclaim God's Word to them because of prejudices. Later, the early Christians failed to tell other people groups about Jesus, because of the same mind-set. Perhaps that is one reason why persecution occurred. After the Jews fled from Jerusalem, the gospel spread rapidly to the Gentile nations. In Singapore, I concluded, 'God's blessings that are not used as he directs can be taken away and given to another.'

The apostle Paul was able to say, 'I was not disobedient to the vision from heaven' (Acts 26:19). Are you obedient, or are you prone to doing your own thing? The gospel is about doing Jesus's thing, but it is impossible to do this without a vision or revelation. According to the old saying, 'When the captain of the ship doesn't know where he is sailing, no wind is the right wind!' It is imperative to call upon the Lord, to shut yourself away, pray and listen to what God is saying. 'My sheep listen to my voice; I know them, and they follow me' (John 10:27). Expect to hear God speak. Listen, write down what he says, and then follow his instructions. It is then that you will be blessed. The vision God gives you will keep you going through any pain barriers to the last lap of the race, and on to win the race! People with vision draw others to follow them to fulfil what God has spoken to them about. Do not be discouraged if you do not receive a clear picture to begin with. Link in with another person's vision until your own becomes clear to you. Paul obeyed the general command to go and, on the way, he received specific instructions from the Holy Spirit. Let us do the same.

Coming to terms with the cost of mission

In some parts of the world, the harvest for the gospel is so

214

ripe that the time is *now*, but there are snakes, mosquitoes, fleas and heat! Before setting out on a mission to a foreign country, we need to consider the cost in various areas of our lives and come to terms with it.

Once, in the jungle of Malaysia, I suffered from severe diarrhoea and asked where the toilet was. They just pointed to the jungle! I do not know if it was the thought of the poisonous snakes out there or whether God healed me, but the problem vanished after that! When we were in the Philippines, the water supply only came on for an hour at two o'clock in the morning every second night.

On the same trip, a group of tribal people visited us in our house and God moved in a powerful way among them in salvation and healing. Wonderful friendships were forged but, after they left, the fleas were jumping and biting so we had to scrub and disinfect the room! The conditions are not always five-star, but if you treat missions as an adventure and challenge, God's grace will compensate for every discomfort.

Lack of privacy is something that Westerners find difficult to cope with, but this has to be faced in Asia. People are very curious and will follow when you go to pray, to eat, or even to wash. If you sit outside to have a quiet time, you can easily be surrounded by a group of people asking questions. It may be a wonderful opportunity to witness, but can also prove very frustrating. Jesus had the same problem when he took his disciples away into the wilderness to take time off. Crowds followed and the compassionate Saviour taught and healed them.

'Culture shock'

'Culture shock' is common when visiting unfamiliar territory, and we should be prepared for it. We cannot, and must not, impose our Western culture on other groups, thinking that it is part of Christianity. Rather, we should respect their way of life, adapt to it, and learn all we can from them. It can prove costly, particularly if you do not like their food! I am noted for having an 'international stomach', which goes with my calling of international evangelist. I am very grateful for it!

My wife teaches on cross-culture awareness to each group that we take out on mission. Once, an Indian pastor took the team out to a restaurant for lunch. Each member took a menu to order their food until Joyce kicked them under the table. 'The pastor will order,' she hissed. In that culture, the host or elder orders for everyone. When the meal arrived, the team were invited to help themselves. They did so liberally, not realising that the host and his children would not eat until the team had finished. In the home, the host would always see that his guests' needs were met first and then give an almost imperceptible nod to his children to allow them to eat. After much persuasion, he and his wife would then eat.

The team had to learn to forgo second helpings, think of others, respect the culture, and leave food for the hosts. Is it right or wrong? Neither – just different. If we are there to serve, we must be willing to learn, to adjust and be a blessing to people in a different environment.

Team conflicts

Although emotional pressure can also be a problem on mission, we can mature as Christians by working through the difficulties. Team conflicts have to be recognised and resolved. We have to learn that God's grace is just as effective in adverse conditions as it is at home. Some of our most fruitful outreaches have been the most costly in this respect. So our response to the call should be, 'Lord, here am I, send me.' A decision is made, 'Now I know, watch me go!'

Selecting team members

In selecting a team to go out on a mission, we should follow Jesus's example of much prayer before choosing the people we are going to take with us. Jesus selected his disciples by direct revelation from his Father: 'Come, follow me . . . and I will make you fishers of men' (Matt. 4:19). The best team members are often those who show faithfulness and teachability, rather than the ones who move in power gifts but have not developed the fruit of the Holy Spirit in their lives.

Preparation for a mission

We usually start a mission with a time of fasting before we leave, seeking God together to know his heart and hear his directions. This corporate prayer and fellowship is always a good time for getting closer together and getting a 'feel' for the team.

Often, when there has been repentance in these meetings, faith and anointings are released to enable us to get the job done. Ministry gifts are given by God to be used for others. The anointing on the team leader will come upon those he is training.

Questions that can be asked during this time are, 'What are your expectations for this mission?' (If they are too high, there will be disappointment. If too low, God's perfect plan will not be fulfilled.) Or 'How do you think your gifting and calling can best serve the team?' This question will help in finding out where each team member fits in.

Faith for mission finance

Most of our missions started with little or no money. Our budget requirement for five months in Asia was £15,000 for a team of ten. Some had the necessary money, but most did not – so we started to pray. We then concluded that, if we had to ask the Lord for all that money, we might as well add on 10 per cent to give away, knowing that our consciences would be hurt if we saw tremendous needs and were unable to give.

I taught the team to reach out to a generous God, in faith, and we found that the money came in when it was needed. It was exciting to ask the Lord where he wanted us to give the extra 10 per cent – to missionaries, orphans, churches, individuals and a contribution towards a jeep. What a joy it would bring to our heavenly Father if every team that went out gave away a tenth of their budget! God loves faith.

Faith is easy when there are six weeks to go, but not so easy on the day payment has to be made and there is nothing in the bank! One day I got a telephone call from a friend. 'How much do you need for your team's air fares?' he asked. '£2,500,' I replied. 'There is a group of businessmen here who are willing to give that amount,' answered my friend encouragingly. The money arrived on time, on the day we had to pay the travel agent. But a few days before that, someone had taken me aside and said, 'Hasn't the money come yet? Are you sure you've got this right?' I remember gulping hard before replying, 'Yes, I believe we have got it right.' What a test! Let us not limit God. If he calls, he will provide. We have seen food multiply and we have been transported miraculously from one place to another. When we do not have the resources, God does have them and he will supply us with everything we need to get the job done.

How much of your church's yearly budget is allocated to those unreached people groups? St Mark's Church gave away 10 per cent of all the money that came in to other ministries. That was a lot of money, and periodically, the giving committee would increase that amount. We were amazed to see the Treasurer's report. The church gave 10 per cent more, and the Treasurer reported a 17 per cent increase in money coming in! This pattern kept repeating itself. Most of this money was not spent on reaching unreached people groups, but nevertheless we were moving faithfully in the truth of the revelation we had at that time.

How informed are you on these groups and on what is done to evangelise them? Are you working with others (churches or Christian organisations) to fulfil the Master's command?

'Arise and shine, for your light has come and the glory of the Lord is risen upon you!' The light and glory of God has come, but it is when we arise that it will be seen. Arise and go – make disciples of all nations (people groups) and then the end, Jesus, will come. Hallelujah!

FOR GROUP DISCUSSION

Aim of the chapter
By the end of the meeting, participants will:

1 Have a better understanding of what is involved in going on an overseas mission.

2 Know whether God is calling them to go on a mission.

Key Scriptures
Read and meditate on the following Scriptures. Underline or make a note of verses that particularly speak to you.

- *The call*: Matthew 28:19, Mark 16:15.
  Examples: Luke 10:1, Acts 8:1–40, Acts 13:2–3, Acts 16:1–40.

- *The vision*: John 10:27, Acts 16:9–10, Acts 26:19–20.

- *The cost*: Luke 14:28–31.
  Examples: Matthew 13:14, Mark 2:2 (lack of privacy), Psalm 133 (independence), 2 Corinthians 6:3–10 (physical discomfort and pressure).

- *Equipping*: Ephesians 4:11–12.

Group participation
Respond individually and as a group (as appropriate) to the following questions/prompting:

1 What struck you most strongly from this chapter and these Scriptures?

2 How much – amount and percentage of total budget – has your church spent on mission in the past three years or so for:
  (a) local missions in the locality of the church?
  (b) missions from the church in support of other churches in the United Kingdom?
  (c) missions from the church to other nations?
  (d) gifts to missionary organisations?

If you don't know, guess now, try to find out later, and compare your guess with the actual figures.

Prayer
Pray as a group and individually (as appropriate) the following prayers:

1 Pray for overseas mission groups. Thank God for all that they have accomplished in the past, are accomplishing now, and will accomplish in the future.

2 Pray for (more of) a release of the spirit of evangelism in your church. Pray for (more of) a release of giving to mission in your church and other churches in this nation.

3 Pray that God will send you to other nations, and that he will tell you when and where he wants you to go. Ask him if he wants you to give specifically to the mission field and, if so, to whom. *Write* down what he says to you on all these issues.

Action
Each group member should tell his neighbour (or tell the whole group if it is small enough):

1 What has struck him most forcibly about this chapter and these Scriptures.

2 What the Holy Spirit has said to him (unless it is clearly something that the Spirit doesn't want spoken out loud).

Suggestions for group leaders
If possible, invite someone to speak to the group who has been on, or involved in, overseas mission. It may be a local individual, or a representative from a mission organisation. Make sure they 'earth' their talk by making it personal, practical and 'honest'. (What you don't really want is a slick presentation from a 'regional representative' of a big mission organisation who has never been on mission himself.)

Alternatively, or as well, invite someone from a foreign country (preferably one who needs to know Christ urgently) to tell the group about the cultural differences between this nation and their home country. (*Note*: The least evangelised nations of the world are mainly Islamic or ex-Communist.)

• Do some research into church finances and the demands

221

that church leaders face so that you can answer the (perhaps negative and critical) enquiries and comments of some group members about their own churches' outward giving. Use local churches for this – perhaps your own; perhaps some of the less mission-oriented ones. But research also the mission-giving statistics of some 'successful' churches in your area, or those with which you have personal contacts*. Are there any lessons to be learned? Is there a correlation between outward giving and 'success' in these churches?

• Teach the group how they should respond to feelings of criticism towards their church. Challenge them in the area in which they are critical of others – for example, 'If you aren't paying a tithe, can you criticise your church for not giving away enough?' 'How much time have you spent in prayer in the past three years that God will change the hearts of the churches and increase their giving?' 'How much are you giving into the mission field over and above your tithe to your local church?'

• As this is the last meeting of the group, decide how the group can best be encouraged to put into practice everything it has learnt. Think about, for example, having an 'end of course' party to which everyone who comes *must* bring a non-Christian friend! Consider a banquet, a barbecue, or a 'pot luck Bring and Share' party. It can be indoors or outdoors. You can have music (bring guitars) or a video. Choose a few group members to give

* The author's church – a fast-growing Pentecostal/charismatic church with a membership approaching one thousand, and a growing heart for evangelism – is currently devoting 8.5 per cent of its income to mission. This is divided as follows: 10 per cent is given to other mission organisations; 40 per cent is devoted to United Kingdom missions and outreach by church members; and 50 per cent is spent on keeping individual missionaries in overseas countries.

their testimonies, or invite a 'celebrity' Christian to give
his or her testimony.

Wouldn't it be wonderful to finish the course by seeing
someone brought to the Lord!

CONCLUSION: A WORD FOR LEADERS

How the whole body of Christ must fulfil its potential

Over the years, I have seen many believers struggling to fulfil their potential. Somehow, many never seem to find their niche.

What are the reasons? The major one is the absence of men and women of understanding who will draw out what God has already placed in people's hearts. I believe God has already deposited his call, his gifts and his purposes in many people's hearts: 'The purposes of a man's heart are deep waters, but a man of understanding draws them out' (Prov. 20:5). Deep in people's hearts are gifts that are waiting to emerge and be used to build up the body of Christ. The responsibility of drawing them out falls to those of us who have been called to lead.

The ministry gifts given in Ephesians 4:7 are not given, as I stated earlier, only as an end in themselves, simply to bless people within the four walls of the church building. People are made apostles, prophets, pastors, evangelists, teachers and leaders in order to *equip and train the saints for the work of the ministry* (Eph. 4:11–16).

These gifts are not for the elite; they are for *everyone* who is ready to roll up their sleeves and serve the body

224

of Christ in their own, personal, God-given capacity. All the gifts should be functioning, with their results visible in a 'strong and united' church that reaches out to its community, according to Paul's promise in Ephesians 4.

From what I have experienced, we have been deprived of these ministries for far too long. Now, I believe, God is restoring them to the Church after Satan has succeeded in robbing us of them for many generations. Each decade since the 1950s has seen the re-emergence of one of the fivefold ministries. The evangelist dominated our awareness in the 1950s; the pastor in the 1960s; the teacher in the 1970s. In the 1980s and 1990s, we have seen the offices of the prophet and apostle being restored.

Interestingly, while we are now comfortable with the pastor, evangelist and teacher, we remain distinctly uncomfortable with the titles 'prophet' and 'apostle'.

I believe we will see this unease disappear when these two offices are understood better and recognised. This is partly because we may have observed extreme or foolish examples of these functions. But abuse of these offices will not be rectified by letting them wither; they will reach their full expression only through correct usage.

Why not pray now that God will raise these five ministry gifts in the churches in your area? Pray also that they will learn how to function together to serve and equip the body of Christ. Once these gifts are in place, the Church will rise to its full potential.

At the international level there are already encouraging signs of the fivefold ministry in operation, as churches and organisations work together to be more effective globally.

I think of Peter Wagner's work with the Lausanne Committee, in which prayer groups from different streams of the Church target unreached areas such as the 10/40 window (a geographical area that includes the Islamic belt). There are also mission organisations

225

working together to contact unreached people groups – they pool their strengths, rather than acting as individual organisations possibly duplicating the efforts of others.

Back in the local church, our team at Kingdom Faith has become aware of the need for the leaders to draw out and recognise the gifts, callings and abilities of all our members. The function of leaders is to cause the body of Christ to fulfil its ministry: 'Through [Jesus Christ] and for his name's sake, we received grace and apostleship to call people from among all the Gentiles to the obedience that comes from faith' (Rom. 1:5).

Grace is God's divine enablement to fulfil his purposes on earth. He gives us grace alongside each of our gifts, so when you use your God-given gifts, you will flow in his grace. Many try to do things they are not gifted or called to do, so without God's accompanying grace their efforts lead to failure, exhaustion and unproductiveness. You will flow in those areas you enjoy.

Evaluate what you have done, what you are doing, and stop doing what you are not gifted or called to do! It is time to begin to work with other leaders to recognise the gifts of Christ in the people whom God has brought to your fellowship. Most pastors are used to hearing questions from their people on the lines of, 'Pastor, what are we doing to reach the AIDS victims/the old people/single mothers?'

Quite often people expect the pastor to perform all the different ministries! But no longer is one man responsible for fulfilling the fivefold ministry in his church. A discerning pastor will recognise an individual's passion and motivation (Romans 12 lists motivational gifts) and encourage that person to enter into new areas of ministry.

In our church, God has begun just such a grass-roots ministry movement. People are being encouraged to follow the dreams and visions God has placed on their hearts, and 'ordinary' believers – not leaders – are working in the following areas: prison work; reaching the wealthy ('the up and outers'); visiting old people's homes; hospitality; hospital radio and hospital visiting; street work; visits to the Gatwick Detention Centre (where asylum seekers reside).

We are also seeing many short-term projects emerging: exotic cookery; free breakfasts; Tearcraft sales; puppets; children's dance; teaching English to au pairs; charity car washes; putting a gospel tract on to the Internet. As leaders, this explosion of energy makes us feel as if the cork has been removed from a bottle of champagne!

Not all the ministries bring growth directly into the church, but therein lies the secret. We are interested in extending the kingdom of God, rather than confining our focus to our own numbers.

Our own church will, in any case, grow (and our current growth from 100 to 1,000 in five years is encouraging) because we know that we will, under God's governorship, reap what we have sown. We are sowing people to fulfil God's purposes.

I urge you to find a need in your community, then use what is to hand to fill that need.

Let's finish the great task of reaping the harvest. Then we can truly say, 'This is our finest hour. My life has counted in God's great plan.'

RESOURCES LIST

Tracts

Bridge to Life, The Navigators Great Britain, 1985. Navpress, Adyar House, 32 Carlton Crescent, Southampton, Hants SO15 2FW.

Five Steps to Life, Scripture Gift Mission, Radstock House, 3 Eccleston Street, London SW1W 9LZ; 0171 730 2155.

Don't You Dare Open This Book, Dan Chesney, Kingdom Faith Ministries, Foundry Lane, Horsham, West Sussex RH12 5PX. Tel: 01403 211505.

Christian Publicity Organisation, Unit 6, Garcia Estate, Canterbury Road, Worthing, West Sussex; 01903 264556. This organisation produces excellent seasonal tracts, and tracts from sporting personalities and other famous people.

Sections of the New Testament and individual Gospels: we give these to new believers. Check out your local Christian bookshop.

Taped Teaching Sets

A series of four boxed sets by David Lamb, entitled *Keys to the Harvest*.

The Kingdom Faith Teaching Course by Colin Urquhart. A discipleship course that is ideal for new believers. Tapes plus worksheets are sent free to enquirers. David Lamb uses this with groups or individuals. Tapes may be purchased.

Books

The Holy Spirit and You, by Dennis and Rita Bennett, Kingsway, 1990.

Strategies for Church Growth, by Peter Wagner, Regal Books.

Catch the Vision 2000, by Bill and Amy Stearns, Bethany House Publishers.

Torah Rediscovered, by Ariel and D'vorah Berkowitz, Roots Messianic Resources, 20 Greenwood Road, Crowthorne, Berks RG45 6QU; 01344 773837.

Films/Videos

Viva Christo Rey International Films, 235 Shaftesbury Ave, London. WC2 8EL.

Ian Macormack Testimony, Ian Macormack Videos, Mr Howard Condor, P.O. Box ACT 501, Kingston upon Thames, Surrey, KT1 2ZA.

Audio tape available from Kingdom Faith Ministries, Foundry Lane, Horsham, RH13 5PX.

Jesus of Nazareth, *Chariots of Fire*, *The Hiding Place*, *The Cross and the Switch Blade* and *The Jesus Film* are available from selected Christian bookshops or International Films, The Coach House, 55 Drayton Green, London, W13 0JD.

Jesus, Paul and the Law, by Dwight Pryor, a set of six tapes from Roots Messianic Resources.

Details of the Ken Houts resource list from:

Care Ministries, 9412 Delmar, Prairie Village, KS 66207, USA.

APPENDIX

Community Survey (1)

1 Do you attend church of any kind? Y/N
  Church attended ....

2 Do you watch religious programmes on TV? Y/N
  If not, why not? ....

3 Do you have a Bible? Y/N
  If yes, how often do you read it? ....

4 What do you think is the
  main purpose of life? ....

5 What matters most in your life? ....

6 What do you feel about
  the state of the world today? ....

7 What do you think is the
  main cause of the problem? ....

8 What do you think
  would solve it? ....

9 Do you believe in God? Y/N

10 Who do you think Jesus is? ....

11 Why do you think
    he died on the cross? ....

12 Do you believe that Jesus is alive today? Y/N

13 Do you believe that there is life after death? Y/N

14 Assuming there is life after death, would you like to be sure of a
    place in heaven? Y/N

15 Do you know that the Bible says that 'God so loved he world
    that he gave his only begotten Son that all who believe in
    him shall not perish but have eternal life'?

16 If you could know God personally, would you be interested in
    knowing him?

17 Any other comments? ....

Thank you for your time and may God bless you . . . .

Name and address (optional) ....

....

....

....

....

Age......... M/F ....

Community Survey (2)

1 Do you pray or have you ever prayed? ....

2 Who do you pray to? ....

3 What would you say prayer is for? ....

4 Have you ever had a prayer answered? ....

5 (a) Do you know anyone who prays? ....
   (b) Do they get answers? ....

6 Have you ever prayed for someone in need? ....

7 Have you ever seen/or do you know someone
   who has been healed through prayer? ....

8 Do you believe in miracles? ....

9 Have you seen one? ....

10 Do you need one? ....

Thank you for your time and may God bless you . . . .

Name and address (optional) ....

....

....

....

....

Age.......... M/F ....

Any other comments? ....